The Cost of Intentional Marriage

Developing a Deeper Understanding of Purposeful Matrimony

Esther Solomon-Turay

THE COST OF INTENTIONAL MARRIAGE
Developing a Deeper Understanding of Purposeful Matrimony

A record of this book is available from the British Library.

Paperback ISBN: 978-1-0687144-0-5
e-book ISBN: pending: 978-1-0687144-1-2

Publisher: Authentic Worth
Website: www.authenticworth.com

Acknowledgements and Special Thanks

The writing journey is not a rush; it takes time to express thoughts on paper that is thoroughly read, studied and reflected on. For this reason, I want to thank God for His Faithfulness in trusting me to release my eighth book; The Cost of Intentional Marriage. Not only has this vision come to fruition, but it symbolises new beginnings and moreover, a new surname.

I do not take this topic lightly and am humbled to have received the wisdom and revelation in articulating my words. Writing is a gift which benefits those who read and is used for strength and tenacity to continue the journey, whilst giving back value to the community.

To my sisters in Christ, thank you for your immense love, prayers and intentions towards me in different ways possible. The tears, fasting, quiet seasons and solitude moments were what was needed to get me to where I am today. I have seen and witnessed what it is to have real, authentic friends turned into sisters; even during their busy schedules, they made time to check up on me, arranging visits and interceding in prayers which have truly made life pleasant.

To my family; thank you for your constant love and sticking closer than a brother. My parents, Mr & Mrs Jacob, have been solid rocks over the years up to the planning stages of the weddings. Their hard work, prayers, gifts and contributions have been second to none. My prayer is for God to prosper you both and be in good health and all that has been given to my husband and I will return back to you a hundredfold.

The Cost of Intentional Marriage

To my beautiful siblings; Ruth and Faith, thank you for standing with me during the transition of my single season to a wife. The banter we had over the years and continue to have at present will forever remain in my heart.

To my beautiful late sister; Glory, who would have enjoyed seeing me as a wife; I salute you highly! Authentic Worth Publishing is still standing strong because you gave me purpose to start this vision. Through your life, you have created a platform for others to share their stories authentically and publish a variety of books for the community at large. Thank you for your strength.

To my business communities, networks, clients, customers, visitors and partners; thank you for allowing me to express my story authentically and incorporating it with Authentic Worth; a publishing platform to help authors and creatives write their stories and publish their books.

To Pastor Jonas and my new church family and friends, wow! Words can't express the love invested and deeply shown. We appreciate you all for the love demonstrated onto my husband and I, and the evidence of your care for the Body of Christ will forever be appreciated, and praying you will receive what belongs to you.

My final and special thanks is for my one and only husband; Mr P. E. Solomon-Turay; my confidant and best friend who I thank God for daily. A man of few words and ample wisdom; he is the gift that keeps giving! This book is dedicated to us because a man like you deserves public honour and acknowledgement. You chose me for who I am, not what I have or own. You looked beyond my flaws, mistakes and continually listen to my transparent moments and times where I need a second perspective.

The Cost of Intentional Marriage

When it felt as if I couldn't go on, you stay true to yourself and remind me by your gentle aura that everything is in God's Hands through prayer and submission. I love witnessing who you are becoming day by day, and more importantly, the man God wants you to be for such a time as this. I love and cherish you forever, bestie!

Authentic Worth's Book Library

As you take the time to read our range of books from Authentic Worth's library, our aim is to provide inspirational, relatable and transparent moments shared with the author. We have 8 books published for your consideration:

It's Time to Heal – A woman's journey to self-discovery and freedom.

Completion – From the perspective of brokenness.

From Glory to Glory – Great beauty in seasons of pain; Strong at the broken places.

The Power of a Forward-Thinking Mindset – Breaking strongholds in the mind.

Confident Face – Embracing your authentic beauty.

Abundant Progress – Maximising the gradual steps of the journey.

The Becoming Woman – Transitioning from the season of waiting to intentionally courting.

The Cost of Intentional Marriage – Developing a Deeper Understanding of Purposeful Matrimony.

All signed books can be found on the website at:
www.authenticworth.com/books

Testimonials of Authentic Worth's Services

Since its inception, Authentic Worth has been an illustrative example of how this literary organisation continues to interpret words in both constructing narratives, as well as elevating new authors into the publishing industry. Each idea placed forward by Esther remains relevant to the ongoing and evolving successes of Authentic Worth for its vibrant endeavours in the future – **Julianna A.**

The Authors of our Generation event hosted by Authentic Worth Publishing was truly an inspirational learning journey for anyone who has ever considered writing a book or sharing a story. Esther shared her story and how writing a book can take time, but never give up. Esther writes books to make people better and stronger, truthful and honest. Well done! – **Cllr Kim Powell.**

I highly recommend Authentic Worth's workshops if you are a budding writer or just want to find out more about the process; the workshops are for you. You will not be disappointed! Take the first step, learn or develop your skill. Esther is a fantastic facilitator who knows how to skilfully navigate their workshops in a way that each person feels included, heard and leaves with more than they had in mind. I am a new author and intentionally chose to publish my book with Authentic Worth's services due to Esther and the team's integrity and diligence! Highly recommended! – **Sasha Gay Smith.**

Wow! What can I say? There was something unique about Esther when I first came across her. I sensed within my spirit that she was the one who was going to help me share my story with the world. With a calm and reassuring demeanour, she just blew me away during my 1-2-1 consultation. Esther listened to what I had to say and gave various suggestions I had not thought of for my upcoming book. I went away from the consultation feeling extremely confident knowing that I was in good hands. Esther is extremely knowledgeable and passionate about her work and the individuals she mentors. Following on from the consultation, she has gone the extra mile to show me that she truly cares about me and my story. Esther, you are a rare gem and an inspiration. I am delighted to become a part of your community and I look forward to going on this journey with you. Thank you for making me really understand that all things are possible as long as I believe – **Gifty Kwaku-Addison.**

I have attended a number of Authentic Worth's events, however the Building Personal Confidence and Resilience for Business Success workshop was the first face-to-face event I've attended, and it was phenomenal! Esther provided such valuable insights and information in a way that was clear, concise and easy to digest and take action upon. Esther's approach really encouraged me and others to share our own experiences and learn from each other. Thank you, Authentic Worth for another amazing event! – **Sheryl Sebastiao.**

I want to thank Esther and the team at Authentic Worth Publishing for an amazing service. Esther has been my rock from day one! Constantly giving me encouragement and being my accountability partner. Her guidance and support have been absolutely first class. Her knowledge of publishing is absolutely incredible. I would not have been able to complete my book without her. I fully recommend for anyone who is thinking about writing a book to get in touch. She will hold your hand right throughout the journey – **Des Amey.**

Contents Page

Foreword

Marriage is a prophetic gift wrapped in the mystery of God's tapestry of grace. Two incredible truths emerge from scripture; it is God's idea in Genesis 2:24 and is meant to be a prophetic picture of God's covenant of love in Ephesians 5:25-32. These two glorious and foundational truths underpin what a marriage with Jesus at the centre looks like.

A secure foundation knowing that God loves marriage and is His idea on how we should love each other in a marriage that is meant to prophetically speak to a broken world of the faithful and consistent love of God.

I love the heart behind this book focusing on 'intentional marriage.' It expresses that alongside God's heart and purpose, we need to take responsibility and work hard to intentionally build healthy and prophetic marriages. As I write this, I have been married for 22 years and even after two decades, I am still loving the adventure in the process of becoming a better husband to my wife. There are at least five lessons I have learnt and continue to learn:

Firstly, in the mystery and the waiting, cling to Jesus. I became a Christian when I was 10, but had no real Christian friends or church community to belong to. Due to this, I grew up longing for a Christian girlfriend, and experienced several relationships that compromised my love for Jesus. I look back with a sense of regret and shame, but no guilt, as I am forgiven!

1

The Cost of Intentional Marriage

There came a moment in one of my relationships where I felt Jesus convicting me of the need to trust Him, and made the decision not to get into another relationship unless I felt it could lead to marriage.

I was single for a number of years and these were painful, lonely and incredibly vulnerable seasons for me. If you are reading this and you desire to be married, but have yet to meet someone, feel nothing but compassion and love from me. For those trusting Jesus in the mystery and waiting, my prayer is that you will be deeply satisfied in His love for you. Trust Him, whatever happens; He is enough.

Secondly, don't compromise on who you have prayed for to marry. My dad gave me some advice as a 20-year-old; at the time I thought it was like a fairytale. He said *"If there is any doubt in your heart, then it is probably not right. When you meet the right person, you will know without any shadow of doubt."*

I was struck by his words and the certainty he felt. I continually prayed for three things; someone who I could be best friends with; someone I would be sexually attracted to and lastly, someone who would inspire me to run into all Jesus has for me.

When I met Sian, my wife, she fulfilled all three in a way that I thought was a fairytale. There were nerves in my heart, but I was totally convinced that I loved her and wanted to spend the rest of my life with her. We got together in October 2001, engaged in December and married in August 2002. I love her more today than I have ever done.

The Cost of Intentional Marriage

Thirdly, the key lesson I needed to learn was not to look for my identity or worth in Sian, but in Jesus. In marriage, it is important that we don't use the other person as an emotional crutch or elevate them to a position they should not be. Our wives or husbands are not God; they are not perfect and their view or opinion of us is secondary to His.

My love language is *words of affirmation* and I have had to work hard at building a healthy attitude when Sian encourages me and the times when she hasn't. The key to a healthy marriage is to keep Jesus as the head and make His opinion of us the place of our security and worth, not our spouses.

A fourth lesson is the commitment of knowing the person we are married to, and not try to make them into the person we *think* they should be. In 1 Corinthians 13, Paul lists different characteristics of what love looks like. Although it is written in how a local church should love each other, it is equally true of what the heart posture and attitude we need to have in intentionally building healthy marriages.

For example, we are to love each other through being patient. Paul is not talking about waiting a long time, but the idea of enduring and not giving up. Paul is saying be patient with people; don't rush to criticise.

Being intentional in marriage means we don't allow anger to live in our hearts, but deal with any issues in patience and love. This means we must be realistic about one another and know there will be things that irritate and annoy you about the other person, and you will need to have patience with one another. We are all works-in-progress and are broken people being made whole by Jesus. Being intentionally patient means that we share our hearts with one another and do not allow things to bottle up internally.

As someone once put it: "Patience is counting down without blast off!" A great way of doing this is taking the time each day to reflect on the outrageous love of God towards us and witness His outrageous patience with us. Another characteristic Paul mentions is that "love is not proud." The word Paul used literally means 'puffed up' to do with arrogance. It is about doing and saying things for your own benefit without the concern for other people.

Even in marriage, pride can creep in and become more about us individually than as a couple. We need to work hard to make sure we are actively present for one another, cheering each other on and being of great support collectively.

One principle I have found is not pulling each other down in front of others, even in a sarcastic way. How we speak to each other is so important! A great way to generate this into the rhythm of our lives is to take time and reflect on the humility and love of God, who owes us nothing, and yet in Jesus, offers us everything. In marriage, we pursue the success of each other in mutual submission.

Paul says that love keeps no record of wrongs. Love is full of forgiveness and has no room for bitterness or holding a grudge against one another. As someone once put it: "A good marriage is the union of two forgivers."

The final and fifth lesson is God being the well spring of love and it defines who He is. He is the God who loves the world continuously that He gave His one and only Son. Be intentional in your marriage and keep Jesus at the centre of it all. Take the time to meet with Him together. Take the time to give your marriage to Him and pray for more strength to love one another. Prayer is a spiritual bond through which we receive a heavenly download of fresh love and grace. Pursue, dream and keep it all about Him.

My prayer is as you read this book, you will be inspired by God's heart for marriage and your marriage will be strengthened and will run into all Jesus has for you. May God pour out His grace upon us as we all work hard and intentionally to build healthy marriages now and for the future.

Pastor Jonas Eyles.

Preface

I t will only become a reality when you step out and believe it will happen! The Esther you see today did not arrive with everything put together. She has been pruned and hidden for a season to gradually allow her light to shine.

The Cost of Intentional Marriage brings a beacon of hope to those who truly want the best in preparing for and building authentic marriages. We thrive by serving others when we write our stories and share them in the community for training, education, elevation and encouragement.

It gives me great pleasure to write a book on the theme; marriage, and what is required to steward it well. I wonder how God would choose me when it seems I'm still new to this, but isn't that the same for married couples who have been married longer? Even they have to learn all over again because it is what keeps us teachable and humble. We won't always have life figured out, but we give ourselves the grace to embrace becoming who we have been destined to be.

The pressure to show others we have arrived because our status has changed from single to being in a relationship will make us feel loved for a while; however, not taking into account the inner-work that needs to be done which can cause some form of disappointment for sharing too soon. Instead, we ought to apply the wisdom of building ourselves first through private study and accountability to others in our community.

Marriage is for the mature, the patient, the humble, the sacrificial and purpose-driven individuals who understand that it takes two people to build strong unions. Marriage is a ministry that should be taken care of by two people with God being in the centre. It takes a willing heart to search within and find those areas that need to be surrendered before saying 'I do.' For those who are looking to be a wife or husband in the near future, it is crucial you study and reflect on each page of this book to prepare your mind for what you are going to learn about yourself.

Marriage is God's gift to those who desire it, regardless of external perspectives and opinions. Healthy marriages do exist! A strong bond is not easily broken because the foundational root is secure in the right Source. Now; let's get into to it…are you ready to learn about the cost of intentional marriage?...

Introduction

Two are better than one because they have a good return for their labour: If either of them falls down, one can help the other up. But pity anyone who falls and has no one to help them up. Also, if two lie down together, they will keep warm. But how can one keep warm alone? Though one may be overpowered, two can defend themselves. A cord of three strands is not quickly broken.

Ecclesiastes 4:9-12 (NIV).

Marriage; developing a deeper understanding of purposeful matrimony. There is power in partnership which gradually becomes the unity of progress, legacy and tenacity. Let's start with a few questions before getting into the book:

- Why is marriage important in today's society?
- Is there a basic understanding or concept of marriage?
- Who created marriage, and is it for the purpose of mankind?
- What are you willing to let go of in order to embrace the journey to marriage?

Before entering the union of marriage, it is important to consider the word 'choice' – how it impacts our daily decisions from the individual we choose to marry, to the purpose which both parties contribute in the world. There are many books, resources, tools and other useful information online about marriage, as well as attending single and relationship networking events to prepare.

The beauty of simply being present and enjoying quality time with married couples is a great way to learn and gain wisdom because it is modelled in front of you. In as much as the above statements are true, we understand that marriage is linked to the purpose of The Garden of Eden in Genesis 1.

We see Adam and Eve bonding and deepening their relationship with each other. Their strong connection and commitment led them to multiplying; although sin came in and caused disruption to occur due to the forbidden fruit that should have not been eaten, which we are now facing the consequences in our world today.

The various levels of pain in different circumstances are sometimes, beyond our control. Through it all, marriage may have certain challenges, but it is important to see the full picture of what marriage truly is; God's Divine Covenant between His children.

When two people find purpose, they are fruitful and multiply when done in the right way. If it is one-sided, it becomes difficult to detect and therefore influences our perspectives. There are different seasons life will expose us to; some uplifting; others pruning and very silent. Either way, both are presented to serve a higher purpose. Marriage isn't a quick procedure; it is a lifetime of 'I do's and surrenders' especially in testing times. Well, that is what it should be...

We are not ignorant of the fact that we have a past which triggers the concept of marriage; perhaps seeing how marriage was modelled in the family home, parents either working towards or against each other, a married couple just starting out or opening up to a new way of giving and receiving love.

This all takes time to adjust as each marriage is uniquely created by God. If one is easily influenced by worldly desires, it can open up the door to follow the customs of what is around us, rather than to be transformed by the renewing of our minds (Romans 12:2).

Being ready for what it takes to thrive in marriage starts in the Secret Place. It is the inner work, healing and endurance of an individual who is committed and communicates early on what they expect from their spouse and contributing to the marriage which makes it a more pleasant experience. The Author and Finisher of marriage is the One who created it in the first place; this is our standard.

Love isn't a feeling you put on whenever it is convenient; it is a daily lifestyle emulated through your walk and talk. You must put on love which builds your own ability to be open to change and relate to others. There isn't only one way to love; people give and receive love in various ways including careful words spoken over someone, buying gifts, spending quality time, being present, enjoying the company of your other half, learning to embrace the quirkiness and differences in the opposite sex, and above all, being a mentally-stable individual who adds value in the life of the other person.

I truly believe that being the best version of who you're called to be takes honesty, focus and the ability to look at your own life and dissect the areas that need further improvement or private development. Your character will speak for you in triumphant and difficult moments; however, in order to be a public success, you have to be a private winner without the applaud of crowds. Other times, you will experience seasons of elevation through failure and learning from mistakes exposed, which is a good sign of growth.

We know that taking matters into our own hands can only get us so far, but when have we taken the time to be still and enjoy the present moment? It would be unwise to assume that walking this life alone is the best way to find and have peace. There are moments in marriage where you may need time to recuperate and refresh your mind, but it shouldn't make you isolate yourself from the blessing you once prayed for.

On the other hand, some have firmly chosen to decide not to marry and have their own reasons which should be respected. We are not to judge or look at them as indifferent. Instead, we can take great examples from the Bible of those who were once married and became widows. We know people who have lost loved ones and may find it difficult to move on without their spouse, or trust they will find love again and create new memories. Every journey is unique and should be respected.

Another example is Apostle Paul in 1 Corinthians 7:8-9 which says "if it was his choice, he (Paul) would encourage the singles (unmarried) and the widows to stay unmarried as he did; nonetheless, if they can't control themselves, they should marry, for it is better to marry than to burn with passion."

In my current marital journey, I choose to focus on each day as it comes and what the moments bring. When two people come together, it is a beautiful gift to witness and enjoy; however, it takes the same two people to work it. Before you are a wife or a husband, remember that you are still an individual. When your name was given to you, it wasn't attached to another person's identity.

The journey to marriage takes the form of understanding every part of who you are before giving yourself to another person. To those destined to marry, let me tell you that marriage is a beautiful gift when two people invest in each other. Sowing and reaping are part of the process; when you both come into agreement, it becomes less about one individual and more on collaborative outcomes which leads to fruitfulness – one shall chase 1,000 but *two* shall chase 10,000.

Ultimately, marriage is a representation of God's love for His Bride (the Church) who reflects His unconditional love on earth; in the triumphant moments and challenging times, all seasons are working together for our good (Romans 8:28). Be expectant and open your mind to the intentional cost of marriage being guided by the Author and Finisher of Love. What we ask for is what we are expected to take responsibility with, which is the reason why we are able to write this book and give encouragement that you are capable of being an exceptional husband or wife in your current season.

The cost of intentional marriage will help you constantly work on yourself and be a better advocate for your partner. Marriage constantly exposes the word *collaboration* – growing into being each other's confidantes, building strengths and challenging weaknesses, whilst being committed to the journey. This is who I choose to do life with – Mr P. E. Solomon-Turay.

Are you willing to commit to the cost of intentional marriage? If so, let's dive into chapter 1…

Chapter 1

Marriage...is that you?

The saying of 'be prepared for what you ask for' is vital in the current climate we are in. Occasionally, we may not always know the magnitude of our requests until it comes wrapped in a package that was not what we initially had in mind.

Think about being in a restaurant; you look at the menu as your eyes glean into the delicious food options until you have to make a decision on what to order. On the menu, the description of each meal sounds simple, but when it is ready to be delivered, you are surprised that it is bigger than expected! On the other hand, there are others who are confident of knowing what to order from the start. From a marital perspective, it is agreed between two people to understand the right choices must be made before commitment occurs.

Marriage is beautiful. Let's start with this first. In a world that is becoming increasingly influenced by peer pressure, instant gratification and the influx of advance technology where information spreads at rapid speed, it can be easy to allow what we hear or see to dictate our decisions. We become accustomed to what we think is the right way to pursue our goals; be it personal, professional, relational and even social.

We want to align ourselves with people that look successful and find ways to get on their level without taking into account that the higher you go, the more responsible you must become; nonetheless, you have to handle what is given to you well. We should not forget the moments that made us who we are; the tears we cried to sleep, the several rejections from jobs we applied for, the fear of not knowing what tomorrow holds and the tension building up in ones' heart due to the unknown. Despite the pain these seasons have brought, it has also birthed a new identity of self; that you are more than your past. Everyone has faced challenges in different ways; some deeper than others; nonetheless, it should not deter us from continuing the journey.

When writing this book, thoughts came to mind on how to start. As a woman who got married in November 2023, I took the leap of faith to write about my experiences in marriage. It is easier to gain insights from seasoned married couples who have been together for over 30 years+, but regardless of being a newlywed, I chose obedience over perfection and continued the writing process. I understood that it wasn't about who was qualified or unqualified, but the lives of those connected that God called me to serve.

Getting married is a life-changer for good. To those who have been married longer than myself, you know what I am talking about. Now; let us not take our eyes off the fact that although I am at the beginning stages of marriage, God is continually pouring His wisdom on how to carry myself in the wifehood season. First of all, I would like to take you back to my 7th book called "The Becoming Woman – Transitioning from the season of waiting to intentionally courting."

The importance of a woman in waiting can feel like a constant battle. She wakes up each day feeling like nothing has changed and life is on repeat; wake up, eat, work, sleep. If her mindset is solely focused on what isn't working in her life, she may assume nothing is changing, especially when the wait has been unbearable and therefore, leading to resentment and doubt.

The Cost of Intentional Marriage

I understand the feeling of tension, especially in a generation where social media constantly advertises highlight reels of engagement rings, big houses and a luxury lifestyle aka living your best life, but neglecting the real work that goes on behind the scenes; moments where we struggle and don't always want people to know what we are going through.

Despite the distractions and what we believe is ours, the real work starts within us! We should not use social media as our standard or goal to build our marriages because of how glamourous a dress may look online or how beautiful the interior décor of a house is. Marriage is about building your own home in a way that is pleasant for the Audience of One, your family and those you choose to invite round.

Yes, you are married, but did you assume it was going to benefit you alone? We can't expect marriage to complete us or feel valued; it is a gift two people must nurture and complement. "But this is not what I signed up for!" How do *you* know what you have signed up for if it is always one-sided?

This can be our perception of what marriage should look like and eventually becomes flawed by our limited understanding of what it requires. At times, the opinions of others can be louder than our own choices and will influence how marriage looks in the home.

> **Are the voices in your head getting louder than the voice of God?**

The work it takes to be prepared for marriage will expose you to how healthy you see spiritual, financial, mental and emotional well-being and building yourself to a standard where you enjoy your own company and embrace the current

15

season. I understand where you are because I too have been there.

From the moment I was told of an encouraging message specifically about marriage in 2016, it came to fruition in 2023. Within those 7 years of waiting, my life was being transformed from the inside-out and God was preparing both my husband and I to officially meet. To this day, I now understand why it took 7 years; the number 7 in the Bible represents completion and perfection, and I perceived it as God preparing us both for our marriage season to shine forth. He truly made everything authentically perfect.

While waiting, we should not wait in vain and do nothing. Rather, we ought to utilise the gifts given to us and work towards purpose so that when our spouse is ready to pursue his wife to-be, it becomes easier for him to discern and choose wisely. As God gradually reveals your purpose, you are able to complement and enjoy each other. Marriage brings out the best in two people starting with yourself. Before coming together, there has to be private work done in order to be a public success.

In order to make your own marriage work, it takes mutual understanding and the reminder that you cannot change the other person without changing you; be the first person to acknowledge areas in your life that need pruning. This season can feel lonely when God is working on you, but it is better to be a healthy version of who you are than being someone you are not. This starts with identifying the areas of your character that needs working on. It's in these moments that contribute to healthy development and growth.

An individual who has a servant-leader character is capable of having a successful marriage which emulates internally and externally.

The Cost of Intentional Marriage

To add on this, being a servant does not mean you are less than, and being a leader should not make you treat others unfairly. It is important to know when to be a lion and when to be a lamb. Regardless of where you are on the journey to marriage, it will come with key lessons that will benefit you when taken from a teachable perspective.

The moment you get into marriage, both parties should learn to submit and be open to each other. This takes great grace, and although women are taught to submit to their husbands in Ephesians 5, it does not necessarily mean her thoughts or suggestions should not be taken into account. More on this in chapter 6.

As married couples, we should know how crucial it is to say the right words in moments of anger. The Apostle Paul in Ephesians 4:26-27 puts great emphasis on not allowing any unwholesome talk to come from our mouths, because it is with the mind that everything begins. Even when it becomes difficult in marriage, that is where you remember the promises of staying true, accountable, present, kind and willing to sacrifice and work for the stability of the union.

God's standard of marriage is not to be misused and be taken with great honour. To the married: reflect on how far you both have come and encourage someone who is desiring marriage to increase their faith and waiting period in preparation.

When we ask for marriage, we are exposing our spouses to the hidden parts we hide, the painful experiences encountered and how to be actively vulnerable when the timing is right. When a man shows interest to a woman, it is not for his own gain, but the vision to build a future for the family and start afresh. Marriage is a gift to couples in building each other up and becoming a powerful force in the Kingdom of God, doing His Will and fulfilling purpose.

During the early months into marriage, we celebrated our first Valentine's Day in 2024 and created a collage of my husband and I with four different civil wedding photos. I captioned it as the following: "A husband's love for his wife should be a reflection of the love God has for His Bride (the Church)."

Each day, by Grace, I get to do life with my husband and see the reflection of God in him which gives me ease of mind to know I am in good hands. When a man has his own personal relationship with God, it builds wisdom to know how to pursue a woman. Above all, there is grace to do marriage well even if it becomes difficult overtime. It is achieved through effective communication and the willingness to commit in all seasons.

Women, on the other hand, are the Brides of Christ and therefore, it is important to ensure they honour their husbands as unto the Lord. When a woman knows what she wants in a man, she too must be in a state of full surrender to God, submitting her ideal list, desires and expectations and trusting her season is approaching. Now, let's move on to the components of marriage.

Do you believe marriage is for you and has what it takes to be a good husband or wife? Consider the following questions and answer them to the best of your ability. Be truthful and look at where you currently are in your life to help you answer them:

What practical ways are you working on building yourself?

_____

_____

_____

_____

_____

_____

Are you ready for vulnerable conversations with your husband or wife-to-be?

_____

_____

_____

_____

_____

_____

The Cost of Intentional Marriage

Have you seen enough of your husband of wife's vulnerabilities to build trust?

_____

_____

_____

_____

_____

_____

_____

Are you ready to commit to an authentic relationship leading to purposeful marriage?

_____

_____

_____

_____

_____

_____

_____

For every gift, there is a cost attached to it. How much you believe that gift is worth will cause you to be wise and cherish it well. Your destiny, time and purpose are working together, and doing marriage the right way will bring out the best in you. Speaking of gifts, we know that times and seasons change, including what we are interested in. We evolve and identify with other attributes to our growth when we take the time to know who we are.

Storytime: When my husband and I started dating in 2021, I understood the importance of transparency in our conversations which helped us tremendously in our transition of courting to marriage. My experiences with courting were steady, beautiful, real, and authentic. It was timely, including our conversations, discussing business and work occupations, what we were intentional about and the specific details of building our home and future. Those vulnerable and honest moments were the starting points for building a healthy environment of trust, integrity and honesty.

Marriage is not an excuse to cover up our mistakes. At the same time, we don't want to assume that marriage is the only fulfilling factor to a prosperous life. Although it is a rich gift from God, there will be seasons where difficult discussions must be made. One day, you may be doing very well at work or in your business, and other days you feel tired, drained and lacking direction.

Coming into marriage is being open to new possibilities, new ways of thinking, being open to the dynamic changes to lifestyle, and contributing to each other's growth. It is understandable why some marriages are not as healthy as they should be because the root of the union wasn't initially established on God's Word.

I remember listening to a message on roots and foundations and found it very intriguing. As a woman of faith, I understand the importance of building a solid foundation when being in a relationship, not only in marriage but with my friends and wider community.

One Sunday afternoon, a friend of mine and I went to the park to catch up and chill. As we walked around the park, we saw a very tall tree. As we walked near the tree, we noticed the roots were deep into the soil and nothing could deter it! This reminded me that when storms come in marriage, the foundation of how to navigate it matters highly. I had to remember that despite what happens, God's Grace is sufficient for us and our union is rooted in His Strength.

Maturing to marital greatness is when you are able to persevere and have strong roots. I would ponder with God and reflect on the marital journey so far, not putting pressure on myself to perform, but simply 'be' present and enjoy what each moment reveals to me and my husband. So far, I am enjoying this great gift of having a man after God's heart that I can do life with.

I also realise that what others are going through in one season could be another person's breakthrough. For this reason, it brings a level of ease and humility to remember that God knows the end from the beginning, and what one may seem as challenging, another person is praying for that specific need. This is what continues to give marriages reassurance, especially when we hear different perspectives on how marriage should be. If we not careful, we can be influenced by our personal decisions and ultimately lose confidence in the reason marriage was initially built; on God's purpose.

It is funny how society can place unnecessary pressure (if we allow it to) on what we should become by a certain age or being led by social trends. Even when vulnerable moments come and there is a desire to share how the journey of marriage is going, it takes wisdom and intentional discernment to know who to speak with.

Before bringing people into your marriage, it is vital to apply wisdom on what needs to be resolved with God first. The Secret Place is where you discover whether marriage is for you and learning to listen when He is speaking. There are several ways that wins God's Heart and that is through communication, surrender and submission.

> **There are discussions you want to talk about on the phone, but humility will make you go to the Throne.**

In those moments, you have to take the time to discover who you are and the position God has given you as a wife or husband on a journey. The wedding is a small glimpse of what life will look like on the other side. Despite the expectations we have on marriage, it is important that healthy communication is at the forefront of setting goals together.

When our expectations in marriage seem unrealistic, it gradually promotes unhealthy comparison, looking at how others are living and not realising the sacrifices it took for those marriages to be in a stable position. In a world where we want to be loved, seen and acknowledged, we struggle to be still with our loved ones to understand not only who we are in marriage, but as individuals.

It is important to enjoy the journey and not only endure what comes our way. When we take the time to understand who we are, we become useful tools in marriage rather than hindrances. Coming with high expectations in marriage can cause disappointments, especially if you have not dealt with past traumas. Bleeding on someone else does not make you whole; be true to yourself and work on those areas you have neglected.

It is a cost to carry past burdens into a new season.

As mentioned before, those vulnerable moments where you can be honest with your partner and talk about the concerns will ease your way into enjoying marriage. I can't thank God enough for the way He made my husband with his calm aura; I enjoy the moments where we embrace each other through communication and God's Hand in leading us to plan for the future.

We don't know everything of course, but we are choosing to trust His leading. This is due to our deeply rooted faith and knowing we have worked to gain a level of each other's trust. We know nothing can be successful without acknowledging the Grace God has over us.

To add on this, no matter what we see online, it will never equate to what real-life marriage consists of. Those moments where we can walk to the park and be present with each other is where the beauty of marriage radiates. There is no pressure to perform and we are enjoying each other; that is what matters. It is in God's Presence where we learn and gain a deeper insight on how to steward each other in love, dignity and respect.

"The person you are married to is someone's daughter or son." This is expensive and should not be taken for granted.

During our first month of being newlyweds, we were blessed to have people come to our home, being invited to eat with other families, celebrated our new season, praying and sharing experiences about their marriages with us, key lessons learnt throughout their journey and how we can find ways to serve each other.

So far, it has been an exciting and humbling journey, and although I have been married since November 2023, there is more to learn about myself and my husband. When your expectations are in alignment with God's Will, it becomes easier to understand marriage and the way it should be. This helps to build further communities of honesty and trust.

I get excited when a woman is newly engaged or a man secures his first property. Signs of healthy growth, maturity and preparation for the next level! With new blessings in sight, it requires new ways of thinking and adjusting to each other.

It has taken time for me to unwind from the initial way of doing things. As I recently ponder over the moments of living with my parents, I would wake up each morning at 5.00am for my devotionals during the courting and engagement season, and commit to 5 days of cardio whilst preparing for the day ahead.

I now see the differences in not only being a wife to my husband, but my role has changed including the quality time given to him, the meals we both enjoy cooking, and watching movies and series I would have never come across (*hubby knows what I am talking about…(Anime!)* I always believe that when marriage is looked after between two people, it becomes enjoyable for all. I have given myself the grace to come into this new season to be present and enjoy what each day brings.

Marriage; when done God's way becomes pleasant and lightweight. To tell you how much I have gained from my husband and the transition stages that have brought us together is based on one word; GRACE! Let's dive into what Grace means for the becoming man and woman in their marital season:

- The Grace to be an exceptional wife or husband
- The Grace to be an exceptional friend
- The Grace to be an exceptional cook
- The Grace to be an exceptional listener
- The Grace to be an exceptional prayer warrior
- The Grace to be present
- The Grace to give your husband and wife some time to be alone
- The Grace to invite God into your marriage and not doing things your own way
- The Grace to be still and know that He is God and in full control
- The Grace to be a contributor in word, deed and action.

In as much as it is a gift and blessing to be married, marriage will expose you to who you are, and at the same time, bring out the best in you when you choose to dedicate yourself to it. Marriage is a Covenant which brings God praise as He entrusts this gift to those He knows will multiply and be fruitful because our lives are attached to His purpose.

When we start changing our mindsets from what we desire, relative to diligently loving our spouse through serving and being present, it makes marriage pleasant and enjoyable. In essence, marriage should not only change your character, but the way others see you and how you see other marriages. We learn a lot from other people and this can be reflected positively in our own marriages.

The Cost of Intentional Marriage

Reflection: Who are you becoming in preparation for marriage, and are you in the right mindset to commit? Knowing that marriage is a lifetime commitment will prepare you for the different seasons life will expose you to. Regardless of what happens, remember that building a marriage starts with knowing what you want in the union and working towards it one step at a time. Let this sink in as we dive into Chapter 2… "Be prepared for what you are asking for!"

Chapter 2

Be prepared for what you are asking for

The saying: 'be prepared for what you ask for' comes at a cost. We can see something which looks good, but in the end, if we don't take the time to discern its true intentions, eventually we give up and assume the process was too long. It is important to remember that what we speak in testing times eventually becomes a reality.

'You are who you hang around' is a popular statement and involves choosing whom you desire to be with on purpose and destiny. In marriage, we have to be prepared to visualise where the union is heading towards. Being with someone to fill in the gap of loneliness or to pass time isn't a suitable reason, neither is it mentally or emotionally healthy.

As I am currently embarking on the journey of marriage, I am continuously learning about pivoting and seeing changes of who I am becoming as a wife from a personal and professional perspective. I am amazed when we desire specific blessings but don't take the time to understand the weight they carry and what it requires to sustain it. Overlooking the process and taking shortcuts may feel good for a limited time, but behind closed doors, no one knows what is happening and this is why we need to learn how to prepare for marriage and purpose.

Seeking a life partner is not the focus but to ensure we are mentally and emotionally ready for what it entails. Whilst preparing for the season of marriage, it is important that we become teachable and humble. No one knows what will happen tomorrow and because of this, it enables me to see marriage from different perspectives, especially looking at what I had in mind, relative to what realistic marriage looks like in today's generation.

Let me talk about my parents who have been married for over 40 years+. We celebrated their 40th wedding anniversary in 2022 as well as being engaged in November 2022. I observe the way my parents both work together in partnership of their marriage. I can definitely imagine their courting days were nothing like the days we have in society now! Despite the ups and downs which we go through from time to time, my parents are examples of perseverance and the willingness to pour into each other.

As married couples, you have a responsibility to encourage and work with your spouse to bring out the best in them and encourage their growth to destiny. I believe it is crucial as a married couple to know where both parties are heading. This is not to say we have everything planned out in detail or know the way to go, but vision is what will start the process.

Being prepared for what you ask for takes honesty and the following points should be considered before committing to a relationship:

- What contributing factors do you believe determine you are ready to get married?
- How are you looking after your family at home?
- What practical ways are you preparing yourself for a purpose-led relationship?
- How do you treat people in the community, place of work and business?
- What books have you read to stimulate your mind in preparation for marriage?
- How do you deal with conflict resolution internally and externally?

The Cost of Intentional Marriage

When 2024 began, I made an intentional decision to have quiet time and not become so busy with business, but allow the Holy Spirit to lead my marriage first. January was a quiet month and rather than making it loud, I chose to rest in the promises that God is in full control. Business and Ministry are two desires I am passionate about, but at the time of starting our marriage, God was working in me and making things work in my favour knowingly and unknowingly. It was those quiet moments that made me realise what mattered most, and this was because I chose to surrender and submit my desires to Him.

Rather than making life work according to my timing, I had to pause and reflect on the fact that God exceeded my expectations and personal prayers I desired in previous years, and now I am reaping what has been sown. When you get married, you will understand what I am saying; what you desire will come to pass and that is truly a miracle God alone can open.

I was blessed to learn from other couples who took time off work to unwind, look after their children, leave their jobs and be present with them. This takes faith, especially in the cost-of-living crisis. It is easier to be busy and booked, working long hours to pay bills and put food on the table, but deep down, when you believe God has a purpose for your marriage, nothing will make you fearful.

I took this on board as I admired women who chose to be present with their husbands and children, believing God will provide and meet their needs. The same applied to my husband and I. We know God has so much more for our marriage and it gets us excited that we are doing life together for His Glory.

The Cost of Intentional Marriage

It may feel easy to imitate what others are doing, but what is important to consider is *'if it is in God's Will, it will stand and come to pass!'*

Seeking God for marriage isn't the problem; it is understanding that marriage belongs to God, therefore, you belong to Him and everything attached with it. Preparation for marriage is about surrender and this is a word we struggle with, especially when we don't see the way ahead. We assume life is too slow and makes us uncertain about what the future will hold.

The biggest mistake to make in the season of waiting is holding onto the mindset that nothing will change. Instead, it is the quiet power within that allows God to rise and show Himself to be faithful. Learn to be still and know that He is God. It is easy to ask and seek for a life partner, but the work it takes to maintain marriage comes with a cost. It can be the cost of not having the lifestyle you had in mind when it seems everyone else is being promoted, travelling to various countries, building and investing in properties, securing work and business contracts etc. It is important to erase the thoughts of doubts and worry because everyone will have their time to shine.

When desiring marriage, you are asking God to strip you off what you thought it should look like. Starting a business can also be a reflection of what marriage consists of. I talk about it from my own experiences of running Authentic Worth Publishing.

Having the vision in 2018, I transformed my online blog into a website and used my two books 'It's Time to Heal' and 'Completion' to teach others how to start writing their first book. It continued in 2019 where I hosted four quarterly workshops on different book topics. I learnt the importance of building a healthy community, not only for workshops but having healthy relationships outside of work.

I continued the journey of running a business with no experience until 2020 came and were informed about the Coronavirus. 2020 prepared me to pivot to the next level! I did not expect a quick transformation in such an uncertain season, but was very intentional to embrace steady growth that would keep me accountable to my journey and avoid the pressure of creating a business that looked good online, but neglecting the purpose of why I started.

Starting the vision of helping authors share their stories was an inspiration that came from a place of stagnation in finding a job after university, the loss of my beautiful sister in 2018 and balancing it with discovering who I was becoming in the process. I could not understand why the job search was difficult; however, I persevered and refused to settle and ultimately chose purpose over feelings.

Until you share your story, you are the only one who will assume everyone is enjoying their lives; however, you have to be willing to listen to someone else's story and remember we are all going through different seasons of life. No one is exempt.

> **Are you prepared to come out of your old mindset and step into the new?**

At a 3-day business event in 2022, I was invited to sell my books and services with other business owners. I went to Primark before starting the business session and a woman approached me. At the time, I was newly engaged. She shared three scriptures whilst speaking words of encouragement over me. Little did I know this specific scripture is what is keeping me today:

The Cost of Intentional Marriage

Isaiah 43:18-19 (ESV) reads:

"Remember not the former things, nor consider the things of old. Behold, I am doing a new thing; now it springs forth, do you not perceive it? I will make a way in the wilderness and rivers in the desert."

I remember having a strong smile on my face as I walked out of the store heading to the business event. Sometimes, God will put people in your life you would not expect to speak a word in season and carry you through the next. When Isaiah prophesies about new beginnings, he helps us remember that our expectations will not be cut off.

In reflection, I understand the old can't come into my new season. I am learning so much in this season of being open to new ways of doing things, and although it takes time to adjust, it is worth the tenacity to keep going. This is known as being prepared for what you are asking for; it is when you ask for something that is beyond you and are willing to embrace the key lessons learnt along the way.

Had it not been for obedience, this book would not have been written. Preparing for marriage constantly teaches me to remember that my husband is the head and I am the crown in reference to Proverbs 12:4 (ESV). It says: "An excellent wife is the crown of her husband." I understand there is beauty in allowing my husband to lead us whilst being humble to learn from his wisdom and gentle aura.

The approach of preparing in our individual seasons brought us together at the appointed time and more importantly, submitting our desires to God. Being constantly reminded that marriage is God-ordained will teach us how to prepare wisely by surrendering everything to Him. With His guidance and all-knowing wisdom, there is peace and reassurance in the gradual process.

Notwithstanding, I don't believe anyone has the full answer, and if that were so, it would be quite overwhelming. Coming into marriage with an open mind enables me to prepare for what is to come. Different ways of learning and being adaptable towards each other is what has sustained us thus far.

When it says in Genesis 2:24 that a man shall leave his father and mother and be united to his wife, it starts with intentional preparation. You will know the intention of a man transitioning into a husband when he makes silent moves with the focus on being one with his wife. What you do today has a direct impact on tomorrow.

I did not realise how intentional my husband was at the time we started talking in 2020; the readiness and commitment to not only pursue me, but having a vision for both of us attracted me to him. When a man has a vision for not only himself, but getting his future wife involved, it is as if the man had a direct conversation with God to ensure the right decision is being made before approval.

The openness and calm approach gave me enough courage, strength and the willingness to submit and open my heart to his leading. I intentionally chose to prepare myself by taking healthy breaks to be present, enjoying what each season was exposing me to and building on my personal development. Even though we may think or assume we have it all together in marriage, it is God who sustains the Covenant. Coming this far is only by the Grace of God and emphasising on preparation stems from being committed to God first before entertaining any man or woman.

The Cost of Intentional Marriage

I am mindful this is not because of my good works or performance, but only by Grace. I am a product of God's goodness even at the expense of not having everything together which I am learning to enjoy more and be present with my husband, family, friends and those in my community. We are all on a journey which unfolds gradually and exposes us to various parts of our lives; this makes it beautiful and pleasant. Nonetheless, it can be challenging when the road seems unclear.

In the preparation stages, the fruits of the spirit in Galatians 5:22-23 must be implemented. Let me choose **PATIENCE** in marriage. What is patience? At times, we don't always pass the test and end up re-sitting. Patience in marriage has to do with how we listen and take the time to soak in what is being shared, not rushing to make decisions. One of the core fundamentals in a marriage is how patient you are when decisions are being made.

When your husband takes time to decide what he wants to achieve for the family dynamics, as a wife, do you convince or try to influence other ideas to benefit you? A husband's role is to lead the wife and his family as Ephesians 5:21-28 goes deeply into what the role of a husband is. As wives, we must learn to respect the position our husbands have, allowing him to lead with integrity.

We may not always know what is on our spouses' minds, but the gift we can give them is time to develop and be who God calls them to be, applying grace and patience. This also means bridling your tongue and being intentional about what comes out of our mouth. Above all, remember to prepare for what you ask for because it is a commitment not only onto your spouse, but to God.

The Cost of Intentional Marriage

Reflection: Love is a cost, but it is also a rich gift when used wisely. What you are willing to let go of will open up doors for the new to come in. Those sacred moments start with having a better perspective of yourself. In your personal relationships and time away from socialisation, are you taking the time to work on every part of your life? It is crucial to have quality time for mindset-growth and invest in your wellbeing. As you prepare to study Chapter 3, we discuss the importance of embracing your individuality before being a husband or wife. Let's dive in…

Chapter 3

Before you are married, you are an <u>individual</u> first

Towards the end of 2023 into Autumn 2024, Authentic Worth Publishing held their virtual monthly book series on behalf of The Becoming Woman covering each chapter in depth and discussing them with the community. In particular, the series covered what it means to be a becoming woman in today's generation.

To society, singleness may seem as if there is something wrong with you. There can be an assumption where singles don't always like talking about being alone because of the fear of missing out, looking at their body clock, wanting to fit in and ultimately, not knowing their identity. Nonetheless, singleness is embracing your individuality in confidence knowing you are more than enough.

What does honouring your individualism in singleness look like?

- Singleness is a positive benefit to <u>you</u> before releasing your spouse

- You have time to work on yourself and love who you are deeply

- You have more time to explore, travel and enjoy your own company before the responsibilities starts coming

- God is most pleased when the single man or woman's attention is on Him and not only in what can be gained

- When you focus on building others, doors of relationships will open up for you

- Purposeful dating or courting can only come when one has fully embraced the beauty of singleness
- You have to be a whole individual before being with your spouse – don't transfer broken pieces to another person

- It is not how long you wait, but how <u>well</u> you wait patiently

Before transitioning from a single individual to a husband or wife, embracing who you are as an individual is vital to your daily progression. When was the last time you enjoyed your own company? I remind the community that stillness does not equate to stagnation, but is preparing them for the next season in their lives. If there is anything I will encourage us to enjoy is TODAY. Embrace each moment of it.

Be mindful that what is robbing your peace, joy and quality time is fixating the mind on what has not yet been accomplished. You are intentional about being in a relationship, but refusing to ask yourself what you are learning during the season of singleness can be a determining factor holding you back.

Can you take the time to embrace your own company without the pressure of being in a relationship? Let's consider the 5 following points:

The Cost of Intentional Marriage

(1) Social Media – what is your current relationship with social media like at this time, and how are you using the platforms to embrace the season of singleness without it impacting on who you are?

(2) Instant Gratification – no matter how long it takes, it will be worth the wait. The instant gratified life is not healthy and will cause you to go ahead of yourself without first identifying who you are and what you ought to learn in the process.

(3) An unwillingness to work on self – self-examination and an honest chat with a trusted friend is vital. We need to be open to the changes we experience and learn from them, rather than assume it is the delaying contributor to our level of growth.

(4) Invisible Pride – an unseen but gradual destroyer in the lives of those we love is pride. For the ladies, having a tensed heart against men should not be the answer, and in as much as it's had an impact on some women, depending on the level of disappointment experienced, we should not make assumptions that all men are the same. This is an error that if not corrected on time, will cause you to have the same perspective, expecting nothing to change and not moving ahead.

(5) Fear of Missing Out (FOMO) – 'I am coming up to my 40's and still single – is there something wrong with me!?' – Firstly, where is your approval coming from? Is it from other people telling you who you are or God? When you know who you are, the fear of missing out will not have any room to affect you. Don't use fear as a tool to play small or rush to be with just anyone. You are right where you need to be, even when it feels like nothing is changing.

The Cost of Intentional Marriage

Being prepared for marriage takes a lifetime because you are still evolving and having to unlearn certain ways of handling tasks and navigating the new season. Why do we try and make life what we want it to be and refuse to let God do only what He knows is best?

The pace of your life right now is doing what it needs to do, even if you feel distant from God or haven't yet discovered who you are. No matter how much you desire something to happen there and then, it has to be in alignment to God's Will and timing. Through it all, you have to enjoy the current season you are in without questioning who you are or where you ought to be.

Timing is everything; you are not out of place or losing time even though society may deem that to be so. Being prepared for the lifetime of marriage is not only a gift from God but a precious asset that must be nurtured well. Each day, I am intentional to learn something new about my husband and relate to his way of thinking. As a man of few words and great wisdom, it humbles me when he makes decisions in such a precise manner of timing.

There is a right time for everything to happen, and when you are in the season of self-discovery and examination, it is the moment to be open to what they reveal. The opportunity to position myself for a relationship would not have been possible if my husband and I met before the appointed time. Whilst I was preparing on my end, God was preparing my husband at the same time.

A recent revelation: the beauty of blessings is that God knows us deeply and sees far ahead of what we can't see; therefore, it gives us hope to know that what is for us will not pass us by. This is encouraging to the one who desires to know every detail about their life.

The Cost of Intentional Marriage

Being single is a rich gift that needs to be celebrated and honoured before proceeding to be in a relationship. When the mind has too much going on, it becomes uncomfortable and restless to know everything at once. The question is, can you handle the current level you are on and how can you use it to help others?

When we try to fix or make life become what we want it to be, we gradually start idolising matters and taking them into our own hands which may bring a temporal sense of entitlement and control; however, it can negatively influence ones' character and assume that having everything our way will make us happy. Our impatience to God is not something to be proud of; we need to make sure we take the time to allow Him to work in every facet of our lives without being the one to control every move.

Being a husband or wife is not superior to being single; in order to be a husband or a wife, you have to embrace being fully single without complaining. Enjoying who you are in the process is vital because that is where you are maturing. Your mental and emotional wellbeing are working for you. Before being in a relationship, you have to enjoy what key lessons are exposed to you in that moment.

We can't expect God to only intervene when we face trouble and go back to our old ways of thinking. Being prepared for marriage is learning how to hide yourself in the Secret Place (Psalm 91) and being real. It's not always easy being vulnerable to those associated with us, but we have the confidence to be real with God in our uncomfortable moments to build us up for tomorrow. That is what He wants to do for you. The truth of knowing I can enjoy who I am becoming rather than making it a goal to rush into a relationship brings peace of mind and ease.

The Cost of Intentional Marriage

During my season of singleness, I was intentional about being around like-minded women who understood their purpose and those yet to discover it. For this reason, I encouraged my loved ones to join online events about being whole, reading uplifting books according to their current season, and studying the Word with friends that continually shapes them in healthy relationships with others.

Checking in on our loved ones, especially those we know are vulnerable or quiet can be a great breakthrough to be and feel seen. We want to embrace and bring out the best in those associated with us by allowing them to be authentic, rather than influenced by what other people are saying. When you are single and own your season, you are able to overcome any challenges that tries to provoke you to work in your own strength.

Am I becoming easily accustomed to waiting for what others will say before I accept myself as an individual?

Perhaps you have not created the time to study yourself – sometimes, it can be the most difficult task to do, because to you, everything looks perfect on the surface, so what is there to change? You may have a great paying job, a highly successful business, solid friendship circles, good networks and communities, BUT...not realising all these will never satisfy because when life becomes challenging, there are battles you will have to face alone.

This is not to say it will last forever, but when God sees you are reaching out to people other than to Him in trust, a thorough work will have to be done to get back to the level where you once desired His Presence.

Are you desperate to see change and release the baggage of what has been holding you back? When you do, you eventually start to see yourself from a new perspective and the way He sees you. The decisions you make will no longer be about what others say, but the truth of who you are. When we are complete within, it attracts the right opportunities to come your way; whether that is through an answered prayer, opportunities that 'look' good but won't open for your protection, and being settled in your current season of growth.

When it came to dealing with my waiting season, I was able to invest in further writing and speaking opportunities. These two skills God has and is continually gracing me to do, particularly in workshop and seminar facilitations. Being able to admit when life takes a hit allows God to do what needs to be done.

When our pain needs to marinate, it hits the hardest roots that we have held onto for so long, or we have once defined ourselves in and closed other people out for fear of them seeing how broken we are. You have to get to the stage where despite people questioning your life and why you are still single, it has nothing to do with them. Keep your focus in check.

As men and women of faith, we have the power of the Holy Spirit; our Advocate who teaches us what we need to do and how to step out when our emotions try to control who we are. At times, when we think we are ready for what we desire, we ought to pause and thank God for His patience working in us because what hasn't defeated you is moulding you in the process.

Not everyone will understand the journey you are on, and it is not your job to convince others why you are not yet married. God in His perfect way will promote you when it is time. Enjoy the season of singleness because it is a gift that once you are married, there is no turning back.

One of my favourite scriptures I received towards the ending of 2021 from a dear sister is Isaiah 30:15 which reads: "In quietness and confidence shall be your strength." – When I was informed about this scripture, I took it as a confirming word for the season that I am safely in God's Hands. I didn't need to understand what was happening or how situations would fall in place, but knowing fully that it will happen at the appointed time, and in less than 12 months, my husband proposed in November 2022. This was due to embracing the fact that I enjoyed my time alone with the Lord without the constant pressure we see from time to time on social media.

In those seasons of working on myself, I was fully invested in developing a healthier relationship with my business, finances and building a strong community of people I was able to pour into. I believe when you invest in others, God will choose the right people for where you are going and will invest back into you. We know how fruitful this is for ourselves and those around us, knowing we are making a difference in someone's life, especially when the battles become louder than our faith in God.

During my single season of embracing individuality, I learnt to make peace with enjoying my own company, building my financial literacy, knowledge of the Word and reminding myself that God still sees me. There were key lessons learnt when being single that has contributed greatly to being a wife and how it continually impacts the journey, whilst balancing other areas in my life that I desire to see change in.

I understood that in order to enjoy marriage, I have to trust that God knows what He is doing. Being strengthened in the single season to writing books of encouragement to inspire and influence the upcoming generation has come with great blessings. It takes boldness and confidence to help others to pray and witness many breakthroughs.

In those moments, you have to remember not to be impatient with how God is working on you or others. As you help others identify who they are, remember that God marks every investment you make in people's lives and will bless you for it.

> **You have to talk with yourself when circumstances try to define who you are.**

Running a full-time business is not my identity; I am not defined by what I do, but who I am in God and how He has given me purpose to run the business well and bring joy to others through storytelling and book writing. There were moments where it felt that being complete and having everything in place was what qualified me to be married, alongside having a business that I can work from anywhere; nonetheless, God surprised me in supernatural ways where I didn't have to force anything to happen.

I enjoyed being who I was during the single season, not realising that God used specific people to re-affirm what I was seeking Him for in my private time. In today's society, we have a world that focuses on how fulfilled we are, how much money we *should* be making, what we should have achieved at a certain age and lifestyles we should be desiring to emulate.

It was during my season of being engaged where I was introduced by a wedding tailor about a channel on YouTube called 'Magnify' – a platform and global network focused on empowering ambitious women of faith. During my time of preparing for marriage, I made time to listen to seasoned women in various stages of marital life to embracing purpose, investing in property, dealing with mental health the right way, etc.

All these topics have contributed to the transition of being single to married. Through the Magnify platform, I eventually started seeing patterns of who I was becoming and able to relate with some of the women who were being interviewed by the hosts. Their vulnerability, openness and transparency made me realise we are all going through seasons, but it does not end there.

I was able to identify and write down what was adding to my well-being and what wasn't, which eventually contributed to embracing the woman in me and sharing moments where God was working even when it seemed quiet. I can tell you the silent seasons were real, but so was God's Presence in those stages! It may have been easy to entertain doubt, but I chose to trust and believe because the promises revealed were too good to be a lie.

As you continue reading the book, I marvel in wonder at how the cost of intentional marriage will help someone in their journey of transition. Even if that person is you, I know my contribution in your life has not been by chance. It is to help you in preparing for intentional marriage by knowing who you are first before the ring goes on your finger.

Before I was engaged, the time I had to build my relationships with my close girls, travelling, weekend getaways and being present helped me to embrace my season and got me ready for the exchange.

Have you considered this perspective before? – See the exchange season as 'engaged' and the completion season as

The Cost of Intentional Marriage

'married' – this can also be applied to purchasing a property. Once you are at the stage of completion, it does not stop from there. It is an on-going investment and commitment for both the husband and wife, but before we get to that stage, we ought to embrace our uniqueness and what we bring to our communities. When this happens, we become open to learning from other seasoned couples who have gone ahead of us on what they have learnt throughout their commitments.

There will be moments where being by yourself for a season is healthy for your mind. It is important to take breaks off social media, enjoying your own company and learning more about who you are becoming. As a man or woman who is intentional about being married, a question to ask yourself is: 'would you marry you?'

In other words, do I enjoy being who I am, what I say to myself and most importantly, how I treat myself? Any self-sabotage or low self-esteem must be identified prior to joining your life with someone else's. It takes pure honesty to be real about who you are and the areas you desire to see change in.

Don't accept where you are and settle, but take the time to build your life one step at a time. It may take work to undergo those vulnerable moments where it is difficult, but it is better to understand that being whole in who you are is the first step to freedom and discovery. Before I desired marriage, I was intentional about specific areas in my life that required change. This started with ensuring my mind was in the right place to maintain healthy thoughts.

Practical ways I maintained a calm and sound mind was surrounding myself with the right people who were called to speak into my life with uplifting messages relating to my season. Although I am still on the journey as a wife, there are moments where being in the element of self takes high priority, and with this comes the embracing of your uniqueness.

Reflection: On the journey to healing and self-discovery, it takes boldness to own where you are, but believe you are called for more. To believe there is more is an indication you are determined and expectant for what is to come. As you choose to embrace who you are individually, you will eventually learn how to embrace and handle life collectively. To be the best version of who you are opens the door to embracing each step to purposeful marriage. As a couple, are you prepared to invest in your marriage? Let's find out as we dive into Chapter 4: Invest in your marriage...

Chapter 4

Invest in your Marriage

Remember this; the wedding day is very precious, but only for a moment. Marriage, on the other hand is an on-going bond creating future legacies lasting a lifetime. It takes two people to build a wholesome and fruitful marriage. Being a woman who enjoys continuous learning, I embrace the specific areas marriage exposes me to each day as I continue doing life with my husband. With this being said, a wife desiring to honour her husband should carry out the following skills:

- **Listening** – being able to take heed to what your husband is saying, how he speaks with you including the tone of his voice and when he is ready to speak about a certain topic that requires a healthy level of submission. As a wife, this helps me honour his point of view, and the way he desires to lead our home. The more I listen without interrupting, the more wisdom is being applied to our marriage, therefore making it enjoyable for the both of us.

- **Doing** – actively contributing and participating in your marriage willingly and freely. As a wife, having a heart to serve my husband each day by cooking breakfast, preparing his lunch for work, cleaning the house, giving my undivided time to him and practically supporting him by honouring the leadership of my husband and his role in my life.

- **Being** – there should be a healthy balance with your husband and giving him the space to gather his thoughts. As a wife, being present with my husband

49

includes enjoying what he likes to watch on TV, giving him time to rest, being his safe space, whilst creating a warm environment when he comes home and wants to be with me without any interruptions. In other words, enjoying each other's company by being present.

- **Showing love** – this comes in different ways and shouldn't be seen from the perspective of being one-sided. As a wife, I enjoy saying: 'I love you' to my husband which is essential before he sets off to work and before he sleeps. These three words represent the love Christ has for His Bride (the church); in the same way, a husband is taught how to love his wife, to protect and nurture her and thoroughly speak words of life over everything she does, according to Ephesians 5:25-28 (emphasis added).

During the time I spend with my husband, it reveals great wisdom, knowledge, understanding, and above all; patience with one another. Two people from different backgrounds brings diverse perspectives; when they come together, it births a new way of living. As a married couple, you both create new rules for each other and what you are intentional about seeing in your marriage.

We enjoy new beginnings as it is the opportunity to start afresh and become more open to learning new ways of doing things. I am the reflection of my husband and he is the reflection of me. Seeing unique traits of what the head over the family does confirms that I follow, submit, respect and honour him.

She submits to him and he loves and takes care of her.

The Cost of Intentional Marriage

When it comes to investing in your marriage, you are signing up for how mentally and emotionally stable you both are and will be. Investing in marriage should not feel like a hefty task; it is what we have been given as stewards to look after what is ours and not let it lose value. Your husband has value. Your wife has value.

Both combined births excellence, but a marriage can only be excellent when the husband and wife understands themselves first and secondly, how they present themselves towards each other. A marriage can lose its value when a wife or husband is reluctant to participate in developing the relationship, or become one-sided.

Have you considered this perspective before? I enjoy using business examples to demonstrate the key relationship between the company and the client. The client desires a specific service which has been discussed prior to the 1-2-1 consultation. When the company decides to offer what *they* assume would be suitable that is not in alignment with the client's expectations, the client will be more inclined to go elsewhere.

In your marriage, you have to be intentional about what you sign up for, to the extent that other people's opinions of what should be done or how you should maintain your union should be greatly limited. Whether you are already married or next to be married, it is not all advice that must be taken into consideration. Most of the times, the contributions in our environments can be the great cause of why marriages are dysfunctional and lack intimacy.

There has to be healthy boundaries set in place to ensure the husband and wife are mentally stable in making decisions without it being a burden. When we hear 'God is working on me' we should not neglect the power of this statement. There is grace and mercy given to those who desire to see change in their lives, and this change is not a forceful one. It can take some time.

When you have identified the areas in your life that need working on, you acknowledge it and accept you need help. Acceptance is choosing to make peace with what needs to change and taking responsibility for it. Investing in your marriage should be a wakeup call which causes you to see gradual change and emulate grace in every capacity.

You are not only marrying your spouse, but the entire family and this comes with a price. To add on this, a husband should place healthy boundaries around his family and his wife in particular, ensuring that he prioritises his wife's needs, feelings and spiritual development.

It is vital for unity and oneness to thrive in marriage because when a man leads his wife, it shows strength and the willingness to look after her. I remember listening to a message of what an aspiring husband should become whilst preparing for marriage, and the responsibilities of looking after his wife-to-be just as a father looked after his daughter when she was young and growing up.

A good father will need to assess the man who desires to marry his daughter. In various cultures, there is a popular tradition known as the *bride price* where an amount is paid from the husband's family to the aspiring wife-to-be's family.

Although the father of the bride does not entertain the mindset of 'selling' his daughter, the bride pride is made to ensure the husband-to-be shows commitment and intentionality towards his wife and her family. Each culture will vary with what they provide as the bride price; however, this has been the tradition for many centuries and believing it will continue in the future.

What are your thoughts on bride prices or dowries collectively, and is this part of your culture? Leave your thoughts below:

_____

_____

_____

_____

_____

_____

_____

A husband should continue the responsibility a father demonstrates for his daughter, including how he will commit to looking after her, prior to her leaving the family home and being entrusted in the hands of the husband-to-be who wants to marry her. This is an investment that must be honoured in the presence of family and friends as witnesses. When your wife is seeking comfort and a shoulder to lean on, it is expected for you as the husband to be present and available to hear her out.

When parents have a very good relationship with their sons, they will need to trust his decision to let him go and move on to become one with his wife. In particular, Genesis 2:24 tells us that a man shall leave his father and mother and be joined to his wife, and the two shall become one flesh.

The Cost of Intentional Marriage

Relationships between parents and their children; on the other hand, have different dynamics. We may not know every detail about the families we are marrying into, but what we do know is who we marry plays a *big role* in the future destiny of our lives.

It is important to consider that both families have been brought up differently and carry their own set of cultural dynamics which has shaped them in being who they are and will come with its own set of expectations. Whilst this is true, it is good to know that having healthy boundaries should be applied to ensure marriages can thrive, are balanced and fruitful.

> **What price are you willing to pay to see your marriage prosper and become its best?**

Every marriage you see whether online or in-person, is unique and should be seen from a place of admiration. When your spouse does something you don't agree with, what is the first point of action? Do you pray about it and then speak with your spouse, or end up sharing your thoughts on social media or to a friend?

By now, we should understand that not everything needs to be shared. As divine wisdom continues to flow in your marriage, you must hold wisdom by the hand and use it well, for it is the foundation needed to invest and build your marriage.

Wives, when you invest in self-care including keeping up with the maintenance of your hair, skin, teeth, nails, clothes, etc, you take the time to shop around and find the right items to look good, but when was the last time you treated your husband, even to a spa weekend? Do we still entertain the mindset of gender roles, expecting certain tasks to be done

The Cost of Intentional Marriage

by our husbands alone? Remember that marriage is your own responsibility, and what you see as couple goals on social media should not make you decide how to build you own marriage. Be influenced by creating a wholesome marriage that is suited for both of you.

The pressure to be seen can gradually become a destroying factor if both parties have not worked on their weaknesses internally. The perfect plan God had in mind for your marriage is to be stable, prosperous and wholesome, not bickering or comparing your marriage to someone else's, particularly those you do not know personally.

Although I am not against social media, I do believe married couples should know what to share and how much. Is it to inspire and bring value into the upcoming married community? As you invest in other marriages, you are able to use the tools and resources in applying them to your own union.

There are marriage courses that couples can invest in if they sense the need to do it. At the time of my engagement, my former church Pastor took the time to provide pre-marital counselling for my husband and I, dealing with 10 core sessions on marriage which helped us greatly.

From time to time, I still listen to the recordings and bask in how faithful God has been throughout the entire journey. To say pre-marital counselling is a must prior to marriage should not be underestimated and we do encourage you to start if you haven't.

> **Coming into a new season required me to be open to new ways of doing tasks and gaining wisdom from other married couples, their experiences and what I am currently learning in my own journey of marriage.**

The Cost of Intentional Marriage

During each counselling session, I understood the importance of the ways I relate to my husband and how he relates to me, currently shaping our love and development for each other. Marriage comes in stages and builds gradually which we embrace in the steps of singleness, engagement and being married. Let's take a look further...

Embracing Singleness – during the single season, I was focused on building my faith and development, understanding who I am as a woman and being responsible with the decisions made to attain the next level. I used this season of being prepared to progress in the transitioning of dating to courting.

Preparing for Engagement – in collaboration with courting led to being a fiancé in November 2022. I knew this was a God-ordained union and although it was less than a year of being off the market as Mrs, I enjoyed every moment of what the engagement season taught me prior to preparing for the weddings (we had three!) and our future marriage.

Enjoying Marriage – what is built privately will be revealed publicly. A Godly marriage reflects Christ and His Church. A marriage can only be what it is when two people are invested in it purely from a place of love and good intentions. Marriage says:

- 'How can we work on this together?'
- 'How can we serve each other with our respective gifts?'
- 'How much capacity do we have to give of ourselves?'

This is what continues to help us on our journey of marriage as we continue enjoying each other and investing in areas we desire to improve. To add on this, investing in marriage is about listening to what the Holy Spirit is saying. It is easy to accept anything that comes our way, but without testing what is spoken of, how can we know whether it will enhance or put a strain on our marriage?

Allowing the Holy Spirit into your marriage will sustain and build it to the level where you experience His peace that surpasses all understanding, and being led by the greatest Advocate of all; the Holy Spirit – Philippians 4:7 (emphasis added).

A great book that helped me to prepare for marriage is 'The Power of a Praying Wife' by Stormie Omartian. It is not a book to read once and you put back on the shelf; it is a daily commitment for a wife to pray for her husband's future decisions. I have read this book more than once and every time I study it, I receive different revelations of what I can do to become a better wife and confidant for my husband.

The power of words is how we birth who we are and become.

There are moments in a man's life where his wife's prayers will be what sustains the decisions he makes and protecting them. The influence of a strong and spirit filled woman is a gift that is worth more than rubies and pearls, particularly when she senses danger or an attack about to happen in her family.

As wives, we want to rescue our husbands from what they go through, but there will be moments where giving God the room to step in must be applied, reminding you that it is His battle, not yours. Perhaps there are key lessons God is teaching husbands on what they need to learn from, rather than his wife rescuing him all the time and taking responsibility.

The Cost of Intentional Marriage

It will not be healthy if the wife is doing the role of a husband the majority of the time. There needs to be order and balance. In order to see marriages evolve into what God has ordained it to be, it is allowing the husband to adapt with the challenges he may face and using them as a catalyst to re-invest in the marriage, being the head in prayer, fellowship, building the family's faith, provision and making peace.

We have to learn and embrace the seasons of investing in our spouses, being mindful of sharing each other's burdens in wisdom. Let's make it practical now; over to you...

Whether you have been married for a year or more, what does investing in your marriage look like?

_____

_____

_____

_____

_____

_____

_____

How are you practically taking time out to look after each other when life becomes demanding?

_____

_____

_____

_____

_____

_____

_____

How do you create healthy boundaries in your union whilst making the time to invest in each other?

_____

_____

_____

_____

_____

_____

_____

Reflection: The more you invest in your marriage, the greater it becomes gradually overtime. You don't have to be perfect, but you have to be present. You have the capabilities to build your marriage when you are mentally and financially stable. Are you ready to mature and level up in your marriage? If so, you are on the right chapter coming up next...

Chapter 5

Maturity in Finances and Mental Wellbeing Matters

Maturation is when you are being fully developed from one dimension to another. It is the transitioning stages of becoming and discovering who you are called to be. In marriage, maturation plays a healthy and important role. Both the husband and wife owe it to themselves to develop a mindset of maturation in all seasons of life. According to the Cambridge Dictionary, maturation is defined as "the process of becoming developed mentally and emotionally."

During the season of courting, my husband was very intentional about what he wanted to achieve in the build-up of being married. During my time of seeking God in preparing my husband, there was work to do, starting with my own mindset, knowing what I wanted, setting my standards and non-negotiables, and above all, deepening my fellowship with the Lord. I knew the more time spent in the Presence of God, the more clarity I will have on where He is taking me.

In that season, I wrote my goals and aspirations on what I specifically desired in my husband which included where we wanted to reside and how to get on the property ladder. This was done during the pandemic in 2020 as a single woman who had faith to believe it was possible.

Within the year of 2021, I was humbled and blown away at the resilience my husband took to commit himself to get on the property ladder and purchase our first home. Despite moving from one city to another, it didn't take too long to adjust as I was open to the Holy Spirit's way of doing things. From time to time, I still get to travel for work which is good, and reminded myself that God is in charge of my life and plans. He opened the door for me and will ensure I am able to handle the new season of transition.

Maturation continued developing in me as I chose to remain focused and intentional about other areas in my life I could work on. Discovering songs of exaltation and praise really helped to develop a stronger connection with God and my husband as well. It wasn't only being spiritually strong, but being mentally stable when we discussed several matters, and asking the relevant questions at the right time.

There came a time where my husband noticed the electricity bill going up; we spoke about it maturely without any fuss and came to the conclusion of what practical steps we will put in place to ensure the costs are manageable.

A very attractive character trait about my husband is his calm demeanour in figuring out what to do. It has humbled, yet made me realise how strategic God is for putting us together. I observe carefully the way he makes decisions with such wisdom and ease that he does not linger or dwell on a situation for too long. This is maturity at its finest!

When a man can make decisions with a level-head, you are in safe hands.

There is a tendency that men should somewhat be aggressive to prove their manliness as confirmation of what a real man should be, when in reality, women desire a safe space to be open with her husband and not feel belittled. She knows that even when challenges come, she can rest assure the task at hand will be accomplished.

The Cost of Intentional Marriage

I remember when the MC for our traditional wedding saw my husband in the family home and sent a text message a few hours later saying: "It was good meeting your other half. He seems level-headed and humble." This is someone that only met my husband once. How much more those who have known him for years.

When you are mature, you don't have to announce yourself; people around you will witness and gravitate to it. When it comes to mental health in today's society, it is becoming a prominent discussion to the extent of it being shared in working environments, social media including LinkedIn which is mainly for professional use, and fostering a sense of inclusion and care.

I enjoy that social media is becoming a platform where transparency and vulnerability in wisdom is being shared. No matter who you are or how much has been achieved, we all have a level of mental health including people who are coming out of toxic mindset traits scarred by past situations.

Depending on the time and season of marriage, particularly those who married during their early 20s, 30s or 40s, there are key lessons to learn. It is important to invest in yourself and the journey of becoming, particularly in these tender ages, as they influence your season of growth as you mature.

With age comes wisdom, and for this reason, we need to be intentional about the way we analyse our thoughts and decision-making patterns. Are they coming from a healthy place and will it benefit you as an individual?

I want to briefly touch up on the power of words as it shapes who we are and the journey ahead of us. Ecclesiastes 3:1 reminds us that there is a time and season for everything including when to speak and when not to speak. At times, when we are in a heated argument or expressing our opinions, we should first of all, consider how safe the environment is through discernment. This should be applied during the dating stages which will determine whether both parties are compatible to proceed in courting.

When dating my husband, we took it in turns to speak gradually and build a friendship first by asking about what we do; our occupations, learning about each other, our interests and hobbies. I for one was very intentional about not only learning about my husband, but being emotionally and mentally present with him.

How you establish yourself in knowing each other during the dating stages will indicate how healthy both parties will be in building rapport. It takes time to know someone. We are not unaware that people change because life is uncertain, but it doesn't mean we should not make an attempt to work on ourselves and build on personal development. If there is any skill that should be applied more in our communities is developing our personal growth and being at peace with where we are whilst on the journey of becoming.

Being compatible isn't about what each other likes or dislikes, but taking the time to work on yourself first. When you point at someone, there are three fingers pointing back at you; what does this tell us? That we shouldn't be too quick to speak or become ignorant, and that we have our own weaknesses pointing back at us if we don't take the time to identify it by the root. One of the key gifts God has given my husband is a good listening ear that is receptive to others, knowing when to speak in wisdom.

Silence is golden.

The Cost of Intentional Marriage

No matter how wealthy you are (which does not necessarily equate to finances alone), it's the maturity and wisdom to handle what has been given that will enable you to handle more successes. During my season of becoming, I identified the differences between wealth and riches. With wealth, it is about learning how to sustain what you have for the long-term, whereas riches are short-term and if not used in wisdom can be lost quickly.

This is not to say we need to be reckless with what we have and be irresponsible, neither is it a way to fixate our minds on riches that we forget who we are or define ourselves by how much we have in the accounts.

With finances, on the other hand, this comes with wisdom being applied, especially in marriage knowing when to save, spend, invest and navigate financial wellness together. What was once yours becomes 'ours.' When two people marry, it will impact their financial wellbeing including building a family, changing jobs, business expansion, investments etc; for this reason, a healthy level of transparency must be accounted for prior to making key decisions for family growth.

Prior to being engaged, it exposed me to be more intentional about working on my financial goals, assessing both my income and expenses. For the business community, whether running a business alone or hiring a small team, you will identify that income fluctuates each month depending on the performances of clients being able to pay for your services, and business opportunities that come your way.

I am constantly mindful of how much is being spent as a business owner, how to increase income and reduce expenses, and learning about the different ways to use money to benefit the family home and our writer's community, giving value through workshops and online seminars on specific topics that are trending. It hasn't been easy, but the results are worth it over time through the feedback we continually receive.

There are other ventures my husband and I are trusting God to lead and guide us through, but for the time being, we embrace the beauty of being present and content with our portion because what we could not do, God exceeded both of our expectations. Despite the rising costs we are facing, there is a mature way couples can collaborate together by setting budget-friendly timetables to ensure they are on track.

Speaking about business cashflow to a qualified financial advisor or accountant prior to being married builds trust and the willingness to be open about your spending habits. It is mentally and emotionally freeing for married couples to know what their monthly income and expenses are for the home and other commitments. There have been different views on spending habits for married couples; nonetheless, we have to do what is specifically suited for the family home with ease and peace of mind.

> **No matter the season you are in, being married will require transparency on spending habits and how the finances are being used in other areas.**

Even if you are not earning as much as you used to, or you are in the process of looking for another role, do not be ashamed of this. In my book 'The Becoming Woman' chapter 6 called 'money and savings' emphasise the prime importance of being financially healthy before saying 'I do.' It dives deeper into knowing your numbers and how money can impact a marriage even before it starts.

The Cost of Intentional Marriage

In order to thrive in our finances, preparing for other ways to make money are essential; for example, building your skillset and expanding your gifts to bring more income or enquiring about the promotion currently advertised in your place of work. Create time out of your schedule to discuss financial decisions with your spouse and keep track of your spending habits. These are questions couples should discuss before any commitment takes place. Let us dive in deeper to the following questions that will add value to your mental wellbeing when dealing with finances in marriage:

Prior to marriage, what steps did you take to discuss financial matters with your partner?

_____

_____

_____

_____

_____

_____

As a married couple, what areas are you both working together on in building financial stability?

_____

_____

_____

Can you trust your husband or wife to handle the finances in the family home? If yes, explain why. If no, explain why:

Reflection: Finances play a massive role in marriage, and regardless of how comfortable you enjoy talking about it, the conversation must be discussed in order to build your mental and emotional wellbeing. This comes with submission and having an open heart to learn from your spouse if they are good at handling the finances at home and beyond. If you struggle with submission, chapter 6 teaches on the practical steps of how to do it with grace and ease. The more you let go of what is in your hand, the better it will be in keeping your marriage healthy and wholesome. Ready? Let's go!

Chapter 6

The Power of Submission

What is mine is yours. As exciting as this sounds, it comes with great responsibility to not misuse or undervalue what is given. When it comes to submission, it is a Godly requirement and essential for married couples to thrive and find purpose in doing life together.

Submission should not be seen as a woman accepting everything she hears, opinions or thoughts from her husband; she also has the right to speak when she feels it is necessary and relevant. Nonetheless, as the husband being the leader of the family home, the wife has to ensure she gives an opening ear to what her husband has to say.

With submission, it takes strength, humility and the ability to lay down ones' pride and consider another perspective over your own. At the same time, submission is not where a husband takes advantage of his wife because she is submitting to him, but respects her as she speaks. As a daughter submits to her father when he gives advice, is the same way a husband should submit to her Heavenly Father when making sound decisions.

I found an interesting blogpost written by Lia Huynh about the perspective of submission. When done correctly, it allows the husband and wife to thrive. She expands further and says the husband needs to embrace his role as a responsible leader who respects his wife, and a wife needs to honor her husband's position in a loving and supportive way.

The Cost of Intentional Marriage

She continues that both the husband and wife must admit their mistakes and desires to make it right towards each other, particularly with the help of Holy Spirit's intervention. *Source*: liahuynh.com.

When it comes to submission in marriage, we can see it from two perspectives:

(1) Submitting to God – Regardless of what you do or don't yet have, our first and most important submission is to God. The earth belongs to the Lord and the fullness thereof in reference to Psalm 24:1. Let us view submission from God's perspective. He is not accountable to anyone or anything because He owns us. As He sees and knows our lives from the end to the beginning, our obedience should reflect that through how we honour and reverence Him. My personal submission to God is what opened the door of marriage; it wasn't because I was perfect or did everything right, but was intentional about the decisions I made, collaborating with God, surrendering my desires, and opening my heart to receive His instructions. The more I submitted myself to the process, the more peace I received, confirmed through the Holy Spirit before seeing the physical manifestation. As a married wife, submission indicates your respect and honour to God, and as you submit to Him, it will be easier to submit to your husband.

(2) Submitting to your Husband – A husband that submits, trusts and depends on God is able to take care of and provide for his household. Honouring men in humility and the willingness to admit they don't always have the answers is the first step to acknowledge who owns his life. It makes a man's role fruitful when a wife humbly submits herself without questioning. For this reason, a wife should contribute to a consistent prayer routine alongside her husband as the head of the family. Your husband has to be in a healthy head-space to make relevant decisions that will suit the family dynamics. For the becoming wife-to-be living at home with her parents or independently, what was once a usual routine such as submitting to her father's requests has upgraded to another level in submitting to her husband who runs the family home. This is a new beginning that must be embraced.

There is a transition from honouring your father to submitting to your husband. As the wife is under the authority of her husband, she is accountable to the way she serves and respects him. Depending on how a father-and-daughter relationship has been in the past, this can have an impact on a wife's perception of how she submits to her husband; nonetheless, a woman healed from her past is able to feel safe enough to trust her husband when he leads.

We may be aware of those who didn't have the best start as a young girl growing up to be a woman and having a present father-figure; therefore, it can have an impact on a woman's mental and emotional wellbeing. As a wife, she will have to learn how to let go of past struggles and choose to trust God in leading her husband.

> **Submission in marriage can look different in each home because our environments shape who we become.**

I was intentional about not allowing external environments to dictate how I should submit to my husband. The character and representation of your husband is in sync to the wife's character, including how they both talk, live and communicate. The fruits I have witnessed and seen in my husband's life prior to dating and getting to know each other has convinced me that I am on the right path. I have become a better woman because of my husband, including the way he carries himself, respects who I am and how he relates with others.

Nonetheless, we have to be aware that submission is not about a person agreeing to everything being discussed, but *selectively* choosing what aligns to who they are, and above all, how submission equates to God having the final say. The first priority should always be to ensure that God is in the centre of the marriage and understand why a wife submits to her husband in being a reflection of reverence to God.

I accepted what God was doing in my life as we started to understand each other according to our unique purposes, and how this is reflected in our behaviours and attitudes. I am grateful for the married couples who inspire me to grow in marriage and learn key lessons from.

There is grace to be a respectful and honourable wife to your husband. When he comes back from a long day of work, what is your first point of call? Is it to talk about how your day went or allow him to unwind and rest, whilst preparing the table for dinner?

Wives, what is your most appropriate viewpoint of submitting to your husband, and how is this practically done in your home?

_____

_____

_____

_____

_____

Husbands, do you take into account your wife's thoughts when she is in communication with you?

During the honeymoon season when we came back, I cherish the moments my husband would make us food each day. I don't believe there are specific gender-roles when it comes to fulfilling tasks in the home. If my husband desires to cook, I wouldn't say no; neither should a woman constantly feel pressured to cook for her husband all the time.

These are topics which should be discussed prior to getting married; should a husband or wife take it in turns to cook, or should it solely by the wife's responsibility? Nonetheless, we are all different, and what may work for one may not work for another.

One of the key attributes of a husband who loves his wife is to speak gently and correcting her where possible if the discussion isn't going the way he intended. A husband who is temperate in his approach to communicate his perspective without leading to a heated argument has created a safe space for the wife to be her authentic self, and trusts her husband's final decision.

At the same time, we see in Ephesians 5:21 (NLT) that the husband and wife should submit to one another out of reverence for Christ. It can be easy to focus solely on the wife submitting to her husband, but there is grace and wisdom when both submits to the needs of each other.

This can often be overlooked as our perception of submission should come from the wife; nonetheless, wives have great wisdom that can be implemented in her husband's life knowingly and unknowingly. This makes it pleasant as a selfless act of love to put each other's needs before their own.

> **Submission done God's way will keep the family stable in challenging seasons.**

When I ponder on how Jesus submitted to His Father as He was filled with anguish in preparation for the Crucifixion, we can sense the deep fear and agony He went through, but finally came to the decision when He said "Not My Will, but Yours be done" in Luke 22:42.

During this time, one could imagine the vulnerability Jesus experienced as He depended on His disciples (close friends) to intercede in prayer at His darkest hour, but they slept off {ref: Matthew 26:40}. It was a challenging time, but Jesus kept His eyes on God knowing fully well He will never be abandoned. A good husband will never belittle or leave his wife to figure it out on her own.

The Cost of Intentional Marriage

As a wife, do you struggle to submit and trust your husband without interrupting? Leave your answers below:

_____

_____

_____

_____

_____

_____

_____

Couples will have disagreements, but a mature couple understands the beauty of surrender and dying to self. As the head of the home, the husband is responsible that his decisions made for the family are congruent with what he believes is suited for the family's future according to God's Will.

As a wife positions herself under her husband, she is expressing trust, authority, honour and the willingness to allow him to lead. Above all, the greatest gift a husband and wife can give each other is a listening ear and respectfully making their thoughts known.

Let's practically look at the roles of a husband and wife when it comes to submission:

The **wife** should:
- Respect her husband's authority and decisions despite having a different view. This shows she honours his leadership in her life and is willing to

follow. This builds trust, empathy and a closer connection. A wife can seek the input of her husband and give him the freedom to share from his perspective. Discussions such as finances, business development, ministry and career progression opens new ideas being shared and respects her husband's wisdom and guidance as vital for sustaining their marriage.

The **husband** should:
- Make his wife a top priority – a wife *is* royalty especially when it comes to a husband considering her needs, treating her and showing undivided attention. A man who raises his voice harshly at his wife will cause her to withdraw. A wife's emotions are very important in marriage, and the husband will need to be mentally and emotionally intelligent in relating to and understanding her ways, thoughts and communication skills.

Some of the practical ways I enjoy submitting to my husband is sharing my prayer points being covered. Likewise; when I go through challenging seasons, having my husband pray and speak words of encouragement is another sign of healthy submission, as he presents my requests to God and stands in the gap.

In marriage, a husband's prayer requests are also the wife's concern. This is a good place for openness, discussion and any areas we need further strength in. To add on this, James 5:16 encourages us to confess our wrongdoings towards each other as it produces healing. The more we pray, the better results will show forth.

To the married couples, how consistent are you in the following three submission points:

The Cost of Intentional Marriage

1) **Selflessness** – You are not more superior than your husband or wife, but equal in God's sight. Although I believe God ensures that husbands are equipped to take care of their wives and nurture them, they must learn how to act selflessly by asking questions on how to serve each other well. This is a healthy way of building communication and identifying areas of desire towards each other, ensuring both needs are met to their satisfaction. A one-sided marriage produces one-sided results, but when two people stand in agreement, great results happen.

2) **Sacrifice** – What areas of concern do you hold onto? During my courting season, I was open about my finances with my husband which helped very much to where we are today. My husband is very good with money, and running a full-time business is hard work. Despite it, I made an intentional decision to contribute towards our home whilst it was being renovated. It can be assumed that the wife shouldn't contribute or commit financially until she is confident the husband will pursue her, but because of my submission to God, He gave me peace that the right decision was being made. To see a man who is willing to sacrifice his time, savings, working long hours and planning for a better tomorrow is what sacrifice consists of. It will cost you something to gain a great return.

3) **Humility** – To honour your partner's perspective is vital in conversations. Humility is a gift the Holy Spirit gives to those who ask for it. The radiance of humility will sustain a marriage, making it pleasant for others to be around. There is grace given to be a good wife and husband. A woman who is humble practises submission under the authority of God and

identifies when she makes mistakes to be corrected. A husband who is equally committed and submitted to God knows how to remain humble towards his wife.

To be successful in submission, it is important to ask and identify areas in your life where you struggle in. We may all have differing views of submission, but regardless of what we think it *should* look like, we know emulating Christ in our marriage is the greatest gift given to us. When you are open, you invite the Holy Spirit to guide you with wise counsel and discern other voices that don't align with where your marriage is heading to.

Marriages thrive when we have healthy boundaries with others in our environments, especially those who may give advice, but we are able to choose what is suited for our marriages. When the time is right to build intimacy and personal growth with your spouse, it will make submission pleasant and healthy for the future.

Submission is a gift and when used at the right time, it will help marriages thrive and become what God intended for it to be. Your marriage should encourage and make other people want to build themselves and emulate grace that can't be explained.

How intentional will you be to work together as a union to surrender and choose each other without compromise? To the married couples who have been together for decades; be a prime example of showing grace, honour and respect to each other. Let newlyweds know that they too, can be respectful in their marriages and continue the great legacy and beyond.

The Cost of Intentional Marriage

Reflection: There is only so much your husband or your wife can fulfil, but they should not take the place of God who is our main fulfilment. Let us learn how to submit to each other, knowing we can rest assure of the outcome in God's time, rather than what we want to see instantly. The time is coming to reap the rewards of your submission towards each other. As we progress onto chapter 7, let's learn how to communicate and be committed to each other because it will sustain your marriage.

Chapter 7

Communication and Commitment (The two C's)

As we are towards the end of this book, I want to leave you with this. How intentional are you about seeing change? We want to see several forms of change in our lives, but the question is; are we willing to make the sacrifices in do so? As married couples and those who are about to enter into marriage, how determined are you to see your union succeed and become its best?

There is a grace that comes to couples who make an intentional decision to discuss their goals, aspirations, family growth, financial wealth-building and legacy, which eventually becomes easier with time. In order to build and sustain a successful and healthy marriage, it should not be compromised or rushed.

In a society that triggers us to rush and skip the development stages, a successful marriage ordained and led by God are based on His values, His purposes and the destiny He has for you to fulfil. There are two key components that increase the value and stability of marriage; they are known as 'the two important C's' which are **communication** and **commitment**. Let us gain a deeper insight into defining what they are and how they apply in marriages:

Communication – when a husband and wife take the time to share their thoughts, it becomes easier to build a solid foundation. The root of a successful marriage is being able to express your thoughts in a respectable manner, without compromise or devaluing what the other person is saying. A richer and more fulfilling marriage takes time to study their

79

environments and discern when it is the right time to communicate and share their hearts with each other. We know there is a right time for everything, including conversations that ought to be shared. It should not be solely based on what is in it for one individual, but being patient and mature to take heed to what the other person is saying. The power of communication in every facet of life requires a level of healthy transparency and wisdom shared. Knowing when to talk is paramount to where the marriage is heading.

Commitment – a great lesson married couples will have to learn throughout their journey is understanding the importance of commitment and being practical with it. In all seasons, married couples have to make intentional decisions to devote to each other especially when times are challenging. Unexpected circumstances may occur that opens the door to question what you signed up for. Remember in chapter 1, we spoke about 'Marriage…is that you?' You are signing up for a lifetime of various seasons that can fluctuate at any time, choosing to remain steadfast, even when you may be on the edge of questioning whether you can do this, and reminding yourself why you got married in the first place. Commitment is not giving yourself fully to everything exposed at once; that will be too much to handle. It is making the attempt to understand each other in a way where you can resonate collectively and still stay committed.

Whatever you need to do in order for your marriage to blossom and grow, do it. Nothing could be more important than that.

Perhaps we tend to assume that communication is only based on talking, but it is also being able to listen attentively to what your spouse is saying and taking it into account. We know investing in your marriage entails seasons where communication will be amplified more than others.

The Cost of Intentional Marriage

There are discussions which may not require digging deep into, but where there are intense situations that not only impact one person but the wider family, it should be taken with thoughtful ease and consideration. In those moments, nothing should be said out of proportion or when the atmosphere is not at its best; wisdom will reveal when it is safe to talk.

It will take unsteady emotions to say something which should have been said privately and with respect. There has to be healthy limits and boundaries set in place, because for every word we speak, they matter and it might not have an immediate impact now, but in the future, who knows what is ahead? As a married woman, I constantly have to unlearn and remain teachable to the way my husband is and the decisions beneficial to not only ourselves, but our future family.

> **How committed are you in seeing your marriage thrive in communication?**

I remember moments where we would have intentional conversations about growing a business, having the right work-life balance, discussing financial planning and budgeting; to name a few. We took time to listen and understand our strengths and other areas needed for further development.

These conversations assist in evolving and developing who we are becoming and contributes to being more productive together. The commitment in any marriage is to ask yourself how invested you are in the first place and having the right focus to remain steadfast.

Fostering mature understanding and having grace for each other leads to increased intimacy of love, respect and honour.

The Cost of Intentional Marriage

God has blessed us with couples who have been married for longer periods and we do not take this for granted. At present, we are constantly blessed with several married couples who share moments of their past experiences, having thoughtful and well-intentioned discussions that make us ponder and reflect on our own union.

A book gifted to us for our new season is 'The Purpose and Power of Love and Marriage' by the late Dr. Myles Munroe. The book shares a lot about the importance of communication in marriage and is a guide to help couples throughout their entire journey.

From envisioning how marriage is, to the reality of how it is activated will motivate you to read books that will support your journey. Although my husband and I are still on a journey, we are constantly evolving and allowing each day to naturally unfold on what we need to learn, and it is beautiful.

Owning who you are in the process of becoming is essential to your personal development. When was the last time you had a real conversation where you were able to take time out from work or your business and be present with yourself? We may be eager to be around our spouses, but there will be moments where you question yourself and the contributions made in your own life's walk.

Every day with God's strength, I endeavour to be a better woman, wife, friend, confidant, aunty, business partner etc, in order to see gradual change within the community and beyond. This starts with me.

The decision to show up and be present takes strength, especially when you are not usually an open or extraverted person. Regardless of what happens, *you* have to declare that today will be a good day! Standing and believing in yourself is the greatest gift to your spouse, enjoying who you are and being comfortable to talk about certain seasons that are difficult to express. For the woman who has trust issues because of the past, be honest and ask yourself what responsibilities you will take on board to be better for those around you.

Being your best self means showing up as you, not what others want you to be. Everyone you see or meet is on a journey, regardless of how successful they look on social media or in their occupations; we all have challenging moments.

We need to give ourselves and others the grace to embrace who we are becoming and be intentional on building emotional and mental wellness, owning up to the struggles we face and communicating our feelings in a respectful manner. This level of communication not only helps in marriage, but within our networks and those we are yet to meet.

Life is beautiful when we discuss ideas, share challenges and find ways to work together. I truly cherish the moments where I had the opportunity of introducing myself at networking events when I was single, joining bible study and prayer sessions with my friends and sharing multiple wins in the different seasons that have helped towards my personal development.

The more you communicate, boldness starts increasing and helps you to make the right decisions. This has also built a level of trust with others and extends grace to those who are in the becoming seasons. When you feel overwhelmed, how do you build yourself up? The first step is to admit it and write down your thoughts, see it on paper and work gradually to invest in a better you.

Over to you: how intentional have you been in communicating with your spouse?

_____

_____

_____

_____

_____

_____

How committed are you to being loyal when challenging times happen in your marriage?

_____

_____

_____

_____

_____

_____

At times, it may be easier and more comfortable to not share anything, but when an issue is tugging on your heart and mind, the best way to let it go is to speak freely. I have been blessed to have moments where I have witnessed loved ones sharing their experiences and expressing themselves articulately to their spouses, appreciating them publicly and privately which strengthens marriages further.

As we learn how to communicate better, we become confident in our relationships with others which has a great impact on the journey ahead.

From my husband's perspective, he shares thoughts below on what it means to be committed and how communication has contributed to our marriage thus far:

A necessary component for marriage is to follow through with the decision you have made (in the past). When stating your wedding vows, you make the decision to be committed to the person you are reading them to. At the time you make this decision, it is the present; yet, it is a decision for the future. As a result, it means you must actively choose to continue and commit to your marriage at every step.

When seasons are enjoyable, this decision will most likely be passive in nature; however, when difficulty arises, it will require active participation to continue the decision you previously made through your vows. The commitment you made to your spouse is ultimately a commitment before God; therefore, seek to honour God by honouring your spouse as you remain committed to one another. Ask God for the wisdom and strength necessary, trust Him, and He will provide it for you.

It is a journey to learn effective communication within marriage. As previously mentioned, Esther and I are going through the book 'The Purpose and Power of Love and Marriage' by Dr. Myles Munroe. Within it, he speaks of a principle regarding communication that I had not come across before, but is inciteful and is aiding in our development. As a general rule, communication for men is usually to give or gain information; whereas for women, communication is to share or learn what one is feeling. This difference in approach highlights the reality that men and women are indeed created differently.

Consequently, within the confides of marriage, this can produce different outcomes, even when conversing about the same topic or situation. During this journey, we are learning the ways in which we can effectively communicate with one another as spouses. The reality of all marriages is how it is actually conducted and will differ from marriage to marriage, as each involves two unique individuals with differing attributes that make them who they are.

Although this technically means that no two marriages are the same, the principle for what individuals who are married desire regarding communication, is universal to all: to be respected, considered, heard and valued.

Here are some practical steps to help you achieve this in your marriage:

- *Aim to articulate your point or views in a manner that your spouse can understand.*

- *Where possible, strive to not condescend in times where you hold differing stances to your spouse.*

- *Remember that you are not enemies or against one another. Although simple in knowing as a statement, this truth can be easily forgotten when arguments occur and emotions flare.*

> **As powerful as communication is, learn to maintain eye contact when speaking to each other.**

Having a spouse who contributes in wisdom and carries leadership qualities is based on the openness of two people. The husband and wife are a team; they are one, yet have their own unique abilities. The beauty of commitment is choosing to become more self-aware on how to help each other, knowing it will amplify the union greatly.

We should not entertain fear when communicating with our spouses, especially when great ideas can potentially change the trajectory of the entire family and the future. Learn to be more intentional with your words and how they contribute to the ongoing journey of marriage. It pays off in the long run and helps to advance in your commitment goals. This is what true marriage is based on.

Reflection: In marriage, we should learn how to serve and be available for each other in all seasons. Asking relevant questions prior to marriage is what helps two people embrace new beginnings. These new levels come with a cost of transparency and the willingness to work together as a union in building for a stronger tomorrow. As we finish off our last chapter with embracing new beginnings, we want you to take the time to reflect on the seven chapters above, and what contributions you will make as you embrace the ongoing cost of intentional marriage.

Chapter 8

Embracing New Beginnings

Knowing my prayers came to pass at the appointed time is one of the biggest testimonies to date! It still humbles me that I did not get here by myself, but those God strategically placed in my life to help, support and position me through words of encouragement, confirmations, and consistency in remembering the Secret Place. I have to emphasise that this is truly the best place to be, especially when transitioning into a new season.

Embracing the beauty of singleness turning into engagement, and being a wife will always be one of my greatest testimonies, because there are men and women who still believe their time will come. Anything the Lord blesses you with, learn to encourage others by reminding them of God's Faithfulness to keep His promises.

New beginnings take time, patience and the willingness to commit to the process. I am still evolving on the journey to embracing new beginnings. When handling new beginnings, what is the first thought to consider?

For me, I was intentional about learning and unlearning certain patterns that occurred in my way of thinking, and being open to different ways of doing things which helped me come out of my comfort zone. I am still on the journey of marriage and open to embracing new ways of learning and becoming a better wife to my husband.

Embracing new seasons is about cherishing each moment of your life with the expectation that you are learning and applying wisdom in your endeavours, be it personal or professional. It is choosing not to be hard on yourself, especially when you get it wrong, but remembering there is grace to start anew. This requires rest as it enables you to think better. When we embrace quiet seasons with ease, it becomes more pleasant to enjoy the moment rather than thinking elsewhere.

As each day unfolds, there is an opportunity to ask yourself what you desire to learn from your season, and what is expected of you in the process. In marriage, we must learn how to apply great grace, especially in the beginning stages, remembering that it takes time to unfold and reveal who you are, not trying to be like other married couples, for we are all made differently.

It takes a level of maturity to remember that new beginnings should not entertain an old mindset and use the same method to create a new path for yourself. We can't expect change if we are thinking on the same level, but ought to challenge that old mindset and become better.

Depending on your level of emotional intelligence, you could be further than where you currently are by reminding yourself about the power of renewing the mind as Romans 12:2 encourages us to do so, and open up to new ways of evolving.

New beginnings expose us to more than where we currently are, whether it seems like it or not. At times, new beginnings may feel somewhat stagnant as you are in a new position, but doesn't look as if anything has changed. In the grand scheme of things, each day will present the opportunity to learn from the past and use it to influence the future, and at times, it may cause you to deal with those hidden trauma's that randomly come out in conversations where healing needs to take place.

The Cost of Intentional Marriage

> **Stretching, pruning and being accountable to your own journey will cost you, and although it won't always be comfortable, it will be worth it in the process of becoming.**

Prior to the big move, the emotions I felt when packing my items in the same week I got married made me realise how quick time goes! Seeing my wardrobe getting emptier by the day, my books on the shelf transferred into the suitcases, whilst doing my last-minute appointments for bridal fittings and finally, my room sounding so echoey (it is real!), I started to embrace what the new season ahead prepared me for.

My new beginning started on Monday 13th November 2023; the day I officially moved into our marital home. Approaching our bedroom and unpacking my items sorting out where I would put them, my husband surprised me with the best bedroom set-up with petals, balloons, welcome home signs, gifts; it was just too much!

I literally shed tears of joy and thanksgiving as I looked back over my courting season and said '*this is what it means to wait well.*' We think waiting for a long period of time isn't doing us any good, but it is preparing us for greater than expected.

Now I look back and thank God that He made me wait. I took everything in and praised God for such a thoughtful and caring husband who goes beyond to build up a future for us. The vision and dynamics of life has changed and we continue this journey knowing it will bless someone in the waiting season too.

In December 2023 when I went to visit my family in London for a couple of days, I noticed my initial room was moved around and re-arranged by my brother who has now occupied the room. When I got to the room, I burst out laughing and reminiscing that indeed, there was no looking back!

The moments I had in my former room will forever be cherished, especially the experiences with God, my siblings and the amazing achievements, especially writing and publishing seven books, but it will never compare to sharing my life with hubby.

This was a new beginning that I chose to *intentionally* enjoy. The long walks to Sainsbury's and the park with my sister and brother will forever be cherished deeply, and as much as the moments are still there, being in my new season has opened my eyes to embracing new ways of being. I am in a place of peace, steadiness and being fully present in the moment.

I make an intentional decision to look back over my life and see how far God has brought me and those He placed in my path, whether for a short season or a lifetime of support. It's those moments I cherish deeply as I continue learning more about new beginnings and navigating balance with work and family life, being able to socialise where possible (with good limits), whilst being a present wife who serves and celebrates her husband at the same time. It is all to do with stepping into a new level of strength and enjoying what each day brings.

Every new beginning gives us the opportunity to prepare and be open to enhanced ways of learning. At a time where I was focusing on business growth in the early stages of marriage, I was intentional not to allow the demands to get on top of the quality time with my husband.

The Cost of Intentional Marriage

It is a rich blessing to have a husband who has a mature work-life balance and embraces our new season. For me, that was what mattered; having each day to learn and embrace our unique abilities, whilst creating time for each other.

When bigger responsibilities start coming, it will remind you of the moments where you had free time to cherish each other, so if you do not have a lot of responsibilities at this present time, I encourage you to create new memories with your spouse; go out for date nights, travel the world, be creative with your gifts, skills and talents, learn a new hobby, and above all; love each other deeply.

> **New beginnings do not always need to be announced; the season you are in will announce itself as you continue enjoying all that is exposed to you.**

Embracing new beginnings starts with having a renewed mindset. As mentioned above in Romans 12:2, we know how powerful the mind is and can become a great asset or stumbling block. As married couples, we should be intentional and consistent in prayers and reminding ourselves that God can be trusted, even when life feels overwhelming.

Due to the fact that God has brought us this far, what more is there to be in control of? There are various stages I am currently building on, but the beauty of the present rests in the fact that I can enjoy each moment without the need to be on top of everything all at once. I am content in the season of wifehood, and investing more in who I am becoming and what the process is teaching me. Some of the most practical ways I have found embracing new beginnings pleasant with my husband are demonstrated by the following questions:

The Cost of Intentional Marriage

"Is there anything you would like me to specifically pray for on your behalf?"

"What lessons are you learning at your workplace that you can reflect on?"

"Have you made time to rest and be present in the moment?"

"What are you currently learning in this season with God?"

These are questions that will also encourage and strengthen your marriage more than you would ever know. How many of us practically ask our spouses about their desires, needs or even how their day went? It can be easy to place more focus on needing attention, but to build intentionality and trust for both spouses are when communication comes in and sharing ideas, thoughts and offering prayers, which deepens the commitment towards each other.

In the good and challenging moments, ultimately prayer will keep marriage balanced and healthy to embrace new beginnings. Each day with your spouse is a new beginning, just as His mercies are new every morning as the writer of Lamentations says in 3:23. Let's wrap up with the final few words from my beloved on what embracing new beginnings mean:

By God's Grace, new beginnings will bring about many things you have hoped and desired for. Yet, conversely will bring about things you did not foresee, things you never desired and things you didn't even know you would come to desire. In our natural way of thinking and envisioning things for the future, we expect everything to occur in a linear and straightforward manner.

The Cost of Intentional Marriage

The truth of the matter is that the future is God's domain and He can, will and brings things about in a way we often do not expect. Many unforeseen blessings and changes come to be in seasons of new beginnings; some immediately and others, over time. Regardless of how life may currently be, we should thank our Eternal Father, depend on Him, trust Him, and actively ask that He leads us in the seasons of life we are in and will be entering.

Reflection

As you ponder on your journey into marriage thus far, what sacrifices will you consider making? We get excited when the breakthroughs come, but the work it takes to build a healthy marriage will require the right character, integrity, environment and a patient spirit that will be tested in several seasons in life.

Marriage works effectively when the Author of love is in the centre of it all. There shouldn't be any pressure to work in your own strength, but learn to lean on God for divine intervention to get you further. There is a cost to marriage, just as Jesus took our place on the Cross and shed His love for mankind, what are you willing to share and lay down to build a fruitful marriage? It takes two people to agree and make it work, regardless of how long it takes.

Because we do not see what is ahead of us, we become easily accustomed to stay in one place. When you desire a specific gift, skill or breakthrough, it takes positioning and believing it will happen, even when you don't see anything change. Your faith is what will sustain you in these moments and it's been what has kept me on the journey of marriage.

As you continue your own journey, remember why you started in the first place; what made you intentional and willing to do life with your husband or wife, and why is it important now more than ever to work as a team?

For those desiring a stronger and fruitful marriage, be gentle with yourself and analyse your thoughts to ensure they are coming from a healthy place and not broken experiences. Build on your own character development and share the challenges with your spouse to build consistent strength together. There is beauty in vulnerability with your spouse; I guarantee it! No one can be successful on their own and it will take a level of transparency to seek guidance and receive support.

> **How intentional you will be in marriage will cost you; the question is, how willing are you to sustain it?**

Remember that no matter where you are in your marital journey, always learn to give grace to one another; we know perfectionism does not exist in a broken world, but two people who are intentional about working as a team will always find inner joy and happiness to thrive and glow.

The cost of intentional marriage will help you embrace each day with your spouse, building a healthy future together and becoming stronger than you were yesterday. Be kind to yourselves and be gentle with your words, because they produce the fruit you speak. Your marriage should be a reflection of character, integrity, loyalty and love being in the centre of it all. The consistent emphasis on forgiveness and moving forwards gracefully is essential to the union.

We have enjoyed writing our experiences in marriage and believe this book will continue to enlighten and help you reflect on your own marital journey. If you know someone who is preparing for marriage, or those who are currently married, get this book as a gift, reminding them that they are loved, cherished and cared for.

Each chapter will help you to be accountable on the journey of marriage and the investments it will take to continually commit. No matter the challenges, keep your focus on the Author and Finisher of love; He will sustain you throughout the season and keep you in perfect peace {Isaiah 26:3}. With much love and grace; the Solomon-Turay's.

Useful Resources

- **Alpha Course – Stay Curious** – https://alpha.org.uk

- **Engagement and Marriage Preparation** - https://www.eden.co.uk/christian-books/family/engagement-and-marriage-preparation/

- **Six tools for Healthy Communication in Marriage** – Focus on the Family - https://www.focusonthefamily.com/marriage/6-tools-for-healthy-communication-in-marriage/

- **Resources on Marriage** – Desiring God - https://www.desiringgod.org/topics/marriage/all

- **Temptations Common to Marriage** – Article by Bobby Scott from Desiring God - https://www.desiringgod.org/articles/temptations-common-to-marriage

- **The Marriage Course** – Want to prepare for your future together? - https://www.themarriagecourse.org/course/the-pre-marriage-course

- **Keys to a Stronger Marriage** – Joyce Meyer - https://www.joycemeyer.org/study/keys-to-a-stronger-marriage

- **God's Design for Marriage (2024)** – Focus on the Family - https://www.focusonthefamily.com/marriage/gods-design-for-marriage/

- **John Piper** – Preparing for Marriage (Help for Christian Couples PDF) -

https://document.desiringgod.org/preparing-for-marriage-en.pdf?ts=1554405003

- **John Piper** – To men who want to marry; how to prepare to lead well – https://www.desiringgod.org/articles/to-men-who-want-to-marry

- **John Piper** – Marriage in Three Postures; how to cultivate and protect trust - https://www.desiringgod.org/articles/marriage-in-three-postures

- **Melody Alisa** – How we're preparing for Christian marriage – https://www.youtube.com/watch?v=yVN9Or8Gw4w

- **Upward Christian Dating** – A woman's guide to preparing yourself for marriage – https://www.appupward.com/post/marriageguide

- **Focus on the Family** – What can you do to help your Christian marriage thrive? - https://www.focusonthefamily.com/marriage/what-can-you-do-to-help-your-christian-marriage-thrive/

Some of the above links have been written in the past couple of years, and still have an impact on our present society; they all have been carefully selected for the purpose of this book and for your consideration. Take the time to go through them with your spouse and find time to discuss it with each other.

References and Further Bible Study

References:

Mental Health of Older Adults (Oct 2023):
<https://www.who.int/news-room/fact-sheets/detail/mental-health-of-older-adults>

What does it mean to be a submissive wife? (2021)
<https://liahuynh.com/what-does-it-mean-to-be-a-submissive-wife-in-a-christian-marriage/#:~:text=Submission%20looks%20like%20respecting%20your,your%20own%20point%20of%20view.>

Further Bible Study:

- **Ephesians 5:21-28** – Submission and Reverence

- **Ecclesiastes 4:9-12** – Two are better than one

- **1 Corinthians 7:2-9** – Avoiding temptation

- **1 Corinthians 13:4-8** – What is Love?

- **Galatians 5:22-23** – The Fruits of the Spirit

- **Proverbs 12:4** – A wife of noble character

- **Proverbs 14:1-35** – The contrast between Wisdom and Folly

- **Proverbs 18:22** – He who finds a wife

- **Proverbs 31:10-31** – Proverbs 31 Woman

- **Genesis 2:18** – God making woman a helper to the man

- **Genesis 2:24** – When a man leaves his father and mother

- **Matthew 19:5-6** – Two becoming one

- **1 Peter 3:7** – Showing respect and honour to the woman as the weaker partner

- **Hebrews 13:4** – Marriage is honourable

- **Isaiah 62:5** – Bridegroom rejoices over bride

- **Colossians 3:14** – Put on love

- **Songs of Solomon chapters 1-8** – A love letter

Recommended books on Relationships and Marriage

- **Not Yet Married** – Author Marshall Segal

- **Things I Wish I'd Known Before We Got Married** – Author Gary Chapman

- **The 5 Love Languages** – Author Gary Chapman

- **The Power of a Praying Husband** – Author Stormie Omartian

- **The Power of a Praying Wife** – Author Stormie Omartian

- **The Power of a Praying Woman** – Author Stormie Omartian

- **I Almost Ruined My Marriage** – Author Eno Jerry

- **The Becoming Woman** – Author Esther Solomon-Turay

- **For Women Only** – Author Shaunti Feldhahn

- **When Women Pray** – TD Jakes

- **The Purpose and Power of Love and Marriage** – Author Myles Monroe

- **Relational Intelligence** – Dr. Dharius Daniels

- **Battlefield of the Mind** – Joyce Meyer

- **Wholeness** – Author Touré Roberts

Connect with Authentic Worth Publishing

Connect with us on our social media platforms:

YouTube: Authentic Worth

LinkedIn: Authentic Worth

Instagram: authenticworth

Thread: authenticworth

TikTok: Authentic Worth

Facebook: Authentic Worth

Website: authenticworth.com

Manuscript Submissions:
submissions@authenticworth.com

General enquiries: info@authenticworth.com

Authentic Worth Publishing is bringing worth back into you through storytelling and book writing!